For Ryan + Ashl[*illegible*],

with great love,

[signature]

A Suicide Note
A Murder

A Rabbi's Obsession with Death,
Loss and Renewal

by

Rabbi Philip Graubart

DEVORA
PUBLISHING
JERUSALEM ◆ NEW YORK

A Suicide Note, A Murder:
A Rabbi's Obsession With Death, Loss and Renewal
Published by Devora Publishing Company
Copyright © 2008 by Philip Graubart. All rights reserved.

EDITOR: Sorelle Weinstein
COVER DESIGN: Ari Binus
TYPESETTING & BOOK DESIGN: Koren Publishing Services
EDITORIAL & PRODUCTION MANAGER: Daniella Barak

Hard Cover ISBN: 978-1-934440-14-8

E-MAIL: sales@devorapublishing.com
WEB SITE: www.devorapublishing.com

Printed in the United States of America

*This book is dedicated to the memory of my
late brother-in-law, Bill Michaels.*

Contents

Acknowledgments

I'd like to thank the members of Congregation Beth El in San Diego for giving me the time and space to write this book, and try out its methods. Also, many thanks to my wife Rabbi Susan Freeman, and my two sons, Benjamin and Ilan.

PHAROAH'S DREAMS

Nightmares afflict Pharoah. He is plagued by dreams about fat cows, skinny cows, and sheaves of grain, and he can't put it together. It doesn't make any sense. According to Genesis (41:8), in the morning, "his spirit was agitated (*tifa'em rucho*)." Rashi, the great French medieval commentator, translates this phrase as "his spirit became crazed." He went crazy.

But was it really Pharoah's nightmares that drove him crazy? According to the text, it wasn't the dreams themselves that upset him, but rather the fact that "there was no one to interpret them" (Genesis 41:9). Actually, according to Rashi, it wasn't that there were no interpreters – Egypt was hardly lacking in dream interpreters and other magicians – but that there was no one who interpreted the nightmares to Pharoah's satisfaction. As Rashi says about the Egyptian interpreters, "their voices didn't enter Pharoah's ears, and he achieved no easing of spirit from their interpretations" (Rashi to Genesis 41:8). His spirit remained crazed, until the arrival of Joseph, who interpreted Pharoah's dreams in such a way that eased his spirit. Joseph brought an order and sense to the nightmares, and Pharaoh was comforted.

This was not the first time that Joseph had performed such a service. Back in prison, his cellmates also suffered from nightmares

(Genesis 40:5–8). But again, it wasn't the dreams themselves that tormented the baker and the butler (the Torah describes the two as *zo'afim*, meaning "extremely sad"). When Joseph asks what's bothering them, they respond, "We've dreamt a dream *and there is no interpreter.*" The problem is the nightmares don't make sense. There is no interpreter. Joseph comforts them by promising he will interpret their dreams.

What's going on here? For me, the nightmares in these stories symbolize the most difficult times in our lives. Humans are not only pattern-seeking creatures, we're meaning-seeking. When confronted by unpleasant, seemingly random, and baffling events, we are desperate for someone to tell us what it all means. *How should I respond? What does this strange, frightening crisis tell me about myself, my relationships? What and how can I learn from this situation? Why did this happen to me?* The questions often torment us more than the events. Our spirits become crazed; until, that is, we find an interpreter.

The Torah is my interpreter. It's my Joseph. I've had my share of baffling crises, and let's face it, who hasn't? Over the past several years, I've looked to the wisdom of the Torah – the original biblical text and its myriads of Jewish commentaries – to provide meaning, to give an orderly and satisfying response to my various personal crises. This process informs how I respond, every day, to new challenges.

I'm aware, of course, that this is an astonishingly narcissistic way of studying Torah. I'm essentially saying, "The Torah was written for me; it's about my life, my problems." But this is not a new idea. According to a well-known midrash (Exodus Rabbah 5:9), God's voice at Sinai varied according to the capacity of each individual Israelite who was listening. In other words, every Jew at Sinai heard his or her own personal message, their own personal Torah. And, for a long time, traditional Jews have believed in the Torah's infinite elasticity, its quality of generating virtually infinite interpretations. "Turn it and turn it," says Ben Bag Bag in Ethics of the Fathers (5:22), "Everything is in it." If everything is in it, that would include my life. Another way of putting it: if we can say, as the Talmud elsewhere instructs us to say, "The world was created for me" (*Sanhedrin* 37A), we can certainly say "The Torah was written for me."

A quick example, both of how the Torah interprets my life, and the nearly bottomless meanings we can find in many Torah passages. After creating the first man, God says *lo tov heyot adam levado* – "It's not good for man to be alone" (Genesis 2:18). The crucial question in understanding this provocative passage is: what does the Torah mean by *levado*? Most English translations render the word as "alone." According to the Torah, this state of being is flawed; *lo tov*, "not good." At first glance, the phrase "not good" seems like a mild criticism. But the Torah uses the word *tov* – "good" – to confirm most of what God creates. God creates light, land, water, the sun, the moon, creeping things, birds, and mammals, and, after each creation, God looks at the thing, and says "good." "Good" is not just a compliment, it's a stamp of approval, a confirmation of each created thing's right to exist.

So "*levado*," isn't just a flaw, it's a fatal flaw. Being *levado* renders the man unworthy of being created. There's actually a Midrash, a rabbinic legend, in which God creates and then destroys several worlds before finally getting it right with our world. I imagine God destroying those old worlds for one reason: they were *lo tov* – they weren't good. So now, rather than destroy the whole world – or destroy the man – God repairs the flaw by creating Eve. Man is no longer alone. The fatal flaw disappears.

I think this is a fair reading of the text. My problem with it is personal. I don't find being alone a fatal flaw. There are many times when I prefer to be alone. Of course, I wouldn't want to be alone all the time. But I've met many human beings who definitely prefer isolation to company. These may not be happy people, but they're not unworthy of existence. And I value my times of solitude too much to think of them as pointing to any kind of deep, existential flaw.

But maybe the word *levado* doesn't mean "alone." Many translators actually render the word as "lonely." Maybe loneliness – *real* loneliness, desperate loneliness – is the fatal flaw. Loneliness, by definition, is a negative emotion. I may sometimes want and *choose* to be alone, but chronic loneliness leads only to despair. It's a flaw.

Except, that's not quite true. The loneliest time in my life was a period I spent in graduate school, in Israel. I had just broken up with a long-time girlfriend, and felt distanced both from my few English-speaking friends and all my Hebrew-speaking acquaintances (at that point, I didn't have any Israeli friends). When I think back on that time in my life, I grimace, both at my immature, overly dramatic, alienation, but also at the almost paralyzing loneliness – a feeling that eventually chased me away from Israel, and changed the course of my life. It wasn't good, the loneliness. But from a distance of twenty years, I can now say that there was something oddly precious in the feeling. Being *levado* – lonely – wasn't good, but it wasn't fatal. I wrote fiction for the first time. I stared at the stars, and thought about God. I learned to play guitar. The loneliness knocked me out of graduate school, but it also revealed new levels of creativity. I found my poetic soul. I understand that, in retrospect, I'm romanticizing an awful time, but even then, I would never have characterized what I was going through as rendering me unfit to live.

As it happens, Rashi doesn't think *levado* means "lonely," or "alone." Here's Rashi's analysis: "It should not be said that there are two domains: God, among the upper creatures with no peer, and Man, among the lower creatures with no peer." For Rashi, being *levado* makes Man utterly unique, without peer. Godlike. Rashi seems to translate *levado* as radically self-sufficient, "with no peer." So, according to Rashi's reading, God created Eve, not to cure Adam's loneliness, but, on the contrary, to *awaken* Adam's loneliness, to help Adam understand that he was not without peer, that he needed other people. Eve, the new creation, the "helpmate," provoked Adam's loneliness – and in some ways even created it. And it was that loneliness that propelled Adam himself to connect with Eve.

In the same way, on a personal level, the loneliness I experienced in graduate school eventually pushed me to find new friends, and, ultimately, to meet my wife. If I hadn't felt lonely, there wouldn't have been any motivation for me to get married, have a family. Rashi reads the verse as, "It's not good for Man *not* to be lonely." It's good to be lonely.

I'm not claiming that Rashi's reading is necessarily the correct reading, just that it's the reading that works best for me. Rashi's explanation interprets a particularly difficult episode in my life. It helps me understand that time, and gives it meaning.

*   *   *

There's two parts to this book. In the first part, "My Life in Torah," I turn to passages from the Torah, and their interpretations from a variety of classical Jewish sources, to interpret specific crises in my life: my parent's divorce; my first funeral (and my first brush with death); and the death of my father. Although the focus here is decidedly personal, my purpose is not just to tell my story. My aim is to demonstrate a method: how every person can find him or herself in the Torah. My claim is that anyone can blend Torah teachings into their own personal narratives.

The second part of the book, "Torah in Life," consists of short essays on each of the weekly Torah readings (you can sign up for fresh insights every week at *www.congregationbethel.org*). The method here is the same; I use the Torah to comment on universal human dilemmas, such as loss, loneliness, conflict, mortality, alienation, longing. But the style is much less personal. In this section, I attempt to show how the Torah gives meaning to, and interprets, the human condition *in general*. Hopefully the reader can then find him or herself in the vast depths of Jewish tradition. Both sections offer the Torah as an always accessible Joseph, a trusty interpreter who takes the baffling, seemingly random trials in our lives, and gives them back to us as coherent stories, with lessons for the future.

PART ONE

My Life in Torah

Chapter 1

A BLESSING FOR ME

I was ten years old when my older sister Beth first showed me my mother's diary. She'd been snooping in my mother's nightstand – a guilty pleasure I would also indulge in – and, among the stained tissues, lipstick containers, tampons, and scattered change, twelve-year-old Beth had found a stationery box. Lifting the lid, she discovered dozens of crème-colored pages filled with my mother's neat, cramped handwriting. The diary, Beth told me, only went back six months. But it had been quite a six months.

Twenty-seven years later, exactly one month after my mother died at the age of 61, Beth and I – along with my other sister and brother, Amy and Jon – cleaned out my mother's bedroom, including that same nightstand. I peeked in and noticed an identical stationery box. I looked over at Beth, and saw she was carefully going through the dresses in my mother's closet. I'm pretty sure she didn't notice what I was doing. I took out the old diary, lifted the cover, and read a couple of lines. I considered calling Beth over, but quickly changed my mind. I quietly closed the lid, then tossed the diary into a bulging garbage bag filled with my mother's old notebooks, torn photos, and letters. None of us brought the least bit of a pack-rat mentality to this chore. We weren't looking to found a museum, just to clean out her stuff, and get the apartment ready for the estate sale. Two days later, my uncle called to tell me that men had finally come to haul away the garbage. The diary was gone.

The story in the diary starred my mother, my father, and several "other women," mostly Elana Meyers, a dark-haired, married Israeli with whom my father had an affair for over a year. Possibly considering the idea of publishing her diary, my mother named her journal, "Chronicles of a Broken Marriage."

After first finding the diary at the age of ten, I checked in on it at least two or three times a week. Before leaving my mother's room, I would always make sure to place the loose pages in the right order, put the lid back on the stationery box, and set the box in exactly the right spot in the drawer. I never got caught. After that first year, I slacked off a bit, even as my mother slowed her pace of writing. But I continued reading regularly for two more years until I stopped abruptly because of one particularly painful entry.

I call the diary a "story," because in my mind, that was how it seemed to me, and, I think, to my sister as well. It was like a narrative external to our selves, our lives, and our day-to-day activities. I remember that we once compared it to the soap opera we watched every day, "Another World," where the infidelities, heartbreaks, explosions of temper, and betrayals paralleled the world in my mother's pages.

Although Beth and I would sometimes read her diary together, we didn't talk about it too often. At ages twelve and ten, I doubt we had the vocabulary – emotional or otherwise – to articulate our feelings concerning our sinking mother and unfaithful father. But Beth did tell me one time that she was surprised at how little my mother's revelations affected her, and how she continued with her day-to-day activities as if she had never discovered the diary. "I still chase boys," she said, "listen to music, sneak cigarettes." At age ten, those activities were nearly as mysterious to me as my parents' ongoing drama, but I got her point. Beth and I joked about it, lampooned it sometimes with our own writings, shrugged it off, even as, like addicts, we crept back for fix after fix. I played basketball, watched TV, read science-fiction books, and snuck into my parents' bedroom almost every other day while they were both at work, and read my mother's words describing the end of her world.

But I *was* only ten years old, innocent and impressionable. And I read the thing for over two years. I still remember some passages word for word. Even if I managed to incorporate those words – that activity – into what I considered the normal routine of any ten-year-old, reading about my father sleeping with another woman (with other women!) surely wounded me. I do remember some bad dreams, though I don't recall the details. And I certainly remember a sudden change, like the flicking of a switch, in how I saw my parents. After reading the first paragraph in the diary, my mother went from protector to victim – a victim whom I, of course, still loved, but also didn't quite respect. And my father – the villain of the story? I never felt the same way about him again.

As damaging as the other entries were, there were two that left permanent wounds in my heart. The first was the suicide note that I found when I was twelve years old. That discovery began strangely, since I didn't even have to sneak through her drawer to find it. For the first and only time, she left the stationery box out – right on the kitchen table. I walked in to get a drink from the refrigerator, and saw it out of the corner of my eye. I wouldn't have been less surprised to see a rat perched on the counter. I jumped up in surprise. Then, of course, I headed straight to the kitchen table, and lifted the lid of the stationery box. Again, something was off. The pages weren't in their usual neat order; they looked like a deck of cards that had been strewn across the table. Also, instead of the title page at the top of the pile of papers, introducing the reader (me) to "Chronicles of a Broken Marriage," there was a single paragraph written in an angular, childlike handwriting, a handwriting far different from my mother's normal rounded, cramped cursive. I read the paragraph. This is what I recall from memory. *"I can't take it anymore. I'm going to end it. The only reason I haven't done it before now is because of the children. My husband betrayed me. I'm going to end it all."*

I took a deep breath and read the words again. Was this a suicide note? She didn't come right out and say she was going to kill herself. But, in context, what else could "it" mean – the "it" that she couldn't take anymore, the "it" that she would have done a long time ago, if it weren't for her children. But, wait, did she even write the note? This was definitely not her handwriting, though looking at it closely, I began to see a resemblance. The i's were dotted with circles and the t's were crossed so low they looked more like plus signs than letters. Also, this writer had children, and her husband was unfaithful. Even as a twelve-year-old, I knew it was unlikely that some other betrayed wife snuck into our house and stuck a suicide note into my mother's stationery box. My mother wrote it.

I went to my room and shut the door.

To this day, I'm not altogether sure why I did that. Why run away when, clearly, any normal son would run as fast as he could to get help? Part of me, I know, was still in denial. She didn't write it, I repeated to myself. It's not her handwriting. Also, it doesn't *say* she's going to kill herself. Maybe she's just leaving, moving out. Anyway, even if she was planning on committing suicide, how could *I* stop her?

Denial matched the sense of unreality with which I'd always approached the diary. Part of me always saw my mother's writing as a show, a soap-opera, a drama – not at all my real life, where my *real* parents, my married parents, slept in the same room, ate dinner with us every night, pecked each other on the cheek, and chatted and joked with each other with the utmost normality. So it didn't matter whether or not she wrote it, whether or not it was a suicide note. The writer was just a character in a novel. And you don't run for help when a fictional character writes a suicide note. Finally, I do remember confronting an interesting ethical dilemma, one that still makes me blush with shame. If I ran to tell my father, I told myself, I would have to explain how I found the note, why I lifted the lid of the stationery box, and why I read what was written. I'd be caught. In other words, in order to save my mother's life, I'd have to get in trouble. So I hesitated. But, to my credit, not for long.

Less than five minutes later, I left my room and went to find my father. I went to the family room, where I heard voices. Strangely enough, Beth was watching our favorite soap, "Another World," which we had compared to our mother's diary. Beth was annoyed that I had interrupted her, but when I asked her where Dad was, she pointed down the hallway toward the garage. By the time I reached him, I couldn't speak; tears clogged my throat. I grabbed his arm, dragged him to the kitchen, and pushed the note in his hand. I expected him to drop it quickly and rush out, or call the police. Instead, he read the note slowly, carefully, as if it were instructions for defusing a bomb. A crooked half-smile played on his lips, and he put his arm around me. I held on tight. Then he disentangled himself. "I'll go find her," he mumbled, more, it seemed, to himself than to me. Then he walked out the front door.

I returned to my bedroom, shut the door, and climbed into bed. I spent the next half hour in a weird oscillation between denial, and the starkest, most painfully glaring, reality I've ever faced; at least until my mother actually died, twenty-five years later. I imagined life as a motherless child, being raised by a father whose irresponsible behavior had all but murdered his wife. I pictured the funeral, felt the dirt, saw the dark-brown coffin, gleaming in the sun.

But then I quickly told myself that it was all a mistake. She didn't write the note; it wasn't even her handwriting. And how could it be a suicide note if the word "suicide" didn't appear? She didn't write that she was going to kill herself, she just said she was going to do "it," an "it" she hadn't originally wanted to do because of her children, but now she would. Anyway, none of this was happening to me, or to her, or to Beth, or to my father. It was a show, a play, a novel, a story called "Chronicles of a Broken Marriage."

I can't remember which state I was in – denial or reality – when I heard the front door open, along with the sounds of my parents laughing. She was alive.

To punish both of them, I resisted the urge to jump out of bed and greet them. I waited until I heard my own bedroom door open, then I turned, and saw them standing together, smiling. "Back from the dead!" my father announced, and grinned. My mother approached the bed. "What did you think?" she asked. "Did you think I was going to kill myself?" I looked at her. Why on Earth would I think that? Kill herself? How could she even use the phrase? "I didn't know what to think," I answered. She nodded.

Later that day, she told me she'd just been experimenting with different handwritings. The note was just a thing to write, she explained, something she could look at, and study the lines of the letters, curves, and dots. I immediately believed her explanation, without question. It was just a thing to write, the suicide note. It could have been an invitation to a birthday party, or a shopping list, or a mathematical formula. Anything to try out a new handwriting. Surprisingly, she never asked me the question I both expected and dreaded: How did you find the note? Or, what were you doing reading my diary? Or, what else did you read? She never asked, but that was when I began to suspect that she knew Beth and I were reading her private thoughts. I maintained that suspicion for twenty-three years until I found out definitively that I'd been wrong. She never knew. In any case, two days later, I found the stationery box, back in its old place in my mother's nightstand. She kept writing. And I kept reading.

Was my mother really planning on killing herself? I believed the ridiculous handwriting story for an embarrassingly long time. I believed it in college; into my twenties; whenever I reflected on the incident, which wasn't all that often. But today, looking back, I have my own theory. I don't think she was playing with handwritings, but I do think she was playing with the idea of suicide, seeing how it felt to take the first step – writing the note. If that felt right, then she could advance to the next stage – the act itself. But my mother's note was probably preliminary to the preliminary. She wrote a pretend note to see if she could then write the real note. And if she could write the real note, the rest would follow. But she never got past the preliminaries. Maybe my father talked her out of it. Or maybe my reaction to her note convinced her to reconsider. Who knows? I never asked her, and now she's dead.

I found a second wounding entry about two years later, when I was almost fourteen. By this time, my parents had separated, divorced, reconciled, and then separated again (they would reconcile once more, I think, before divorcing a final time during my senior year of high school). I'd cut back my reading to no more than once a week, maybe even less, because as an adolescent, I became even more self-absorbed. Girls, acne, and sports, frankly, loomed larger in my life at this point than my parents' soap opera. Their story grew less interesting to me. Even though there had been more infidelities, more confrontations, more despair, further visits to various counselors, I was past the shock, past the morbid curiosity.

Around this time, Beth and I became even more certain that my mother was writing with an eye to publish. We could see signs of editing: corrections in the margins, cross-outs, paragraph revisions. We also noticed that she'd removed several of the less coherent entries, and had gone back to the beginning, and numbered the pages. You could now read the diary from the beginning and follow a distinct narrative starting with the first affair, then continuing on to separation, divorce, reconciliation, and separation. All that was missing was the ending.

We knew that my father had read parts of it because we heard him discuss the writing with my mother. He appreciated the style, the flow, but suggested a different title. That was another reason why I suspected – wrongly, as it turned out – that my mother knew I'd been snooping through her drawer. Why would she speak openly to my father about it in front of Beth and me if she wasn't tacitly acknowledging that we were all in on the secret? They know we know, I told myself. Pretty soon I would see "Chronicles of a Broken Marriage" on the shelf of a bookstore.

The entry that once again threw me for a loop was part of a general complaint about my mother's life. She was back with my father, but didn't trust him, couldn't sleep easily with him stirring next to her, dreaming about who knows who. Some strange, sordid office politics plagued her at her new job; she had acquired an MA in Library Science, and was now working as a business librarian for a pharmaceutical company. And there were the kids – us. I remember the lines by heart; how could I ever forget them?

"I don't get any satisfaction from the kids," she wrote. That was the first sentence. The next sentence was this: *"The only one I really like very much is Beth."*

It's nearly impossible to remember, much less articulate, the astonishingly complicated jumble of reactions that coursed through me as I read, "The only one I really like very much is Beth." She doesn't like me. My mother dislikes me. I'm pretty sure my first impulse was to erect a defensive shield against this damning statement. "Well, I don't like her very much, either," I thought, with great clarity. "So who cares if she doesn't like me?" The truth, of course, is that the terms "like" and "dislike" played no role in how I thought of my mother; she was my mother; she annoyed me; I loved her; that was it. Until that moment, "liking" was an utterly irrelevant idea. But, as long as she brought it up, then, okay, I didn't like her either!

A different thought popped into my head, yet another defensive reflex: "It's just a *story*." It's a soap opera, a novel, a play. She didn't, I reminded myself, actually commit suicide, because nothing in this so-called diary was real; it was about characters she invented in her tormented imagination. This wasn't my mother disliking me, this was the *character* of the mother, disliking all of her children except for the one coincidentally named Beth.

Ultimately though, these thoughts, much like the ones that I sought refuge in upon discovering the suicide note, didn't protect me. The written words themselves – very clearly in her handwriting – broke down the wall of denial that I had erected, and pierced through my heart. And though I've certainly healed since then, and hardly ever think about the diary anymore, some fragments remain, embedded, stuck.

Before even replacing the page, and putting the lid back on the box, I remembered a recurring dream from early childhood. I'm not certain, but I believe this dream first presented itself around the time I was being potty-trained. Versions of this dream floated through my nightly unconscious for at least three years, until past my sixth birthday. Each time, I found myself crawling up the stairs, toward my mother, who stood at the top, silent, with her finger pointing downward. I was desperate to join her at the top of the stairs, but she clearly wanted me to turn around. And, like in many dreams, I kept crawling, climbing, but didn't get anywhere. The pointing finger seemed to stop me in my tracks. At age six, I didn't know the words "rejection" or "disapproval," but that's what I felt. Now, I don't want to overstate this. For all I know, these were normal feelings for a just potty-trained boy, normal dreams. And after age six, I didn't think about the dreams at all, didn't analyze them, or associate them in any way with my reality as the son of my mother. That is, not until I read those lines in the diary. And then a strange, completely irrational idea popped into my head, which, for years, I couldn't entirely dismiss. "Was it really a *dream*?" It always seemed so real. Maybe it really happened. Maybe one day I actually tried to crawl up the stairs to my mother, but with one crooked, angry finger, she turned me away. Maybe it wasn't a dream at all.

I didn't make a conscious decision at the time, but I never read the diary again. The reasons are complex, but they boil down to this. As difficult as learning about my mother's pain and father's sin was, there was something titillating in their story. It was like snooping through my father's dresser, and discovering old copies of Playboy. It was like eating a forbidden fruit, tempting and tasty, or reading a forbidden text, fascinating and strangely satiating. But reading about my mother's true feelings for me – and, despite my denial, I knew that every damn thing I read was true – was simply too much. I stopped reading, and tried to forget that the diary had ever existed.

And, believe it or not, I mostly succeeded. Acne, girls, and sports, gave way to other teenage pastimes, other anxieties, including grades, colleges, friends, and more girls, so it wasn't hard to turn away from my parents' secrets. Which, anyway, were not really secrets. They kept splitting up. And even though they never told us the reason, did they really think we didn't know? Especially the last time, when they announced their final separation at the same time my father informed us that he was getting remarried. Remarriage, just a month after divorce, to a much younger woman. I didn't need to read my mother's diary to figure out what was going on. In other words, my father's affairs crept out of the diary into the day-to-day fabric of my life, losing their mystique, their titillating quality. So I didn't often think about that part of "Chronicles of a Broken Marriage."

But the other lines flashed through my head at odd times in my life, well into adulthood. I remember one particular time when I was home from college for several weeks, and my brother and sisters were all away. That was a nice time in my relationship with my mother, possibly the best. We would meet for lunch near her office in downtown Cleveland, or go out to dinner, or talk about our love lives (hers was consistently more interesting than mine), or go jogging together. I enjoyed that period, though I couldn't stop one question from beating through my defenses, even at our happiest, most giggling, most delightful interactions: "Does she like me?"

Many years later, my wife and I suffered through two miscarriages. After the second, I phoned my mother. She listened sympathetically, as always, and offered good advice. I cried a little. It was a lovely, loving conversation. At the end, before hanging up, she said something to me that she didn't say very often, though, I never for a moment, even when I found those lines in the diary, doubted that it was true. She said "I love you." Ah, I thought, after putting down the phone. She loves me. But, I wondered, does she like me?

Upon Reflection

Esau and His Parents

> When Esau heard the words of his father, he howled a great and ex-
> ceedingly bitter howl and said to his father, "Bless me, also me, oh
> my father!"[1]

To me, this is the saddest verse in the Bible (not, it must be said,
a particularly happy book). Esau goes on to plead, "Have you not
saved a blessing for me?" When Isaac, his father, answers no, Esau
responds, "Do you have but one blessing, oh my father? Bless me,
also me, oh my father!" And then, "Esau lifted his voice and wept."

Esau weeps because he learned that his brother Jacob, abet-
ted by his mother, has just stolen the blessing that, as a firstborn,
should have been his. But he howls bitterly because his father can't
or won't overturn this clear fraud, and bless Esau. "Behold," Isaac
says, "I have made him your better, and given him all his brothers as slaves, and endowed him with corn and grain, so for you,
what can I do, my son?" In fact, Esau is experiencing one of the
most painful psychological wounds to afflict any human being:
rejection by both parents.

We've already learned that his mother prefers his brother to
him. The text itself dramatizes this motherly betrayal by portray-
ing Rebecca herself as dressing Jacob in Esau's "dainty things" in
order to trick Isaac. The very hands that once dressed her child
Esau in these same clothes now conspire against him. An act of
motherly intimacy becomes an act of betrayal. But now, even
worse, Isaac, his father, who, up until now, had always preferred
Esau, turns against him.

"What can I do?" Isaac says, as if it's entirely out of his hands.
So Esau stands utterly bereft of parental support. His mother never
liked him, and now his strangely powerless father despises him.

---

1. Genesis 27:34.

In many ways, this is a story about flawed parents, about a wound forming through parental misdeeds. Shortly after Jacob and Esau emerge fighting from the womb, we learn that Rebecca favors Jacob and Isaac prefers Esau. The reason the text gives for Isaac's preference is almost comical: "because of the game he [Esau] put in his mouth."[2] Isaac's parental world apparently doesn't extend farther than his own appetite. We never learn Rebecca's precise reasons for preferring Jacob, but we can imagine that his essential traits as "a simple man, a tent-dweller"[3] more closely match her feminine preferences than Esau's – "a hunter, a man of the field."[4]

The Kli Yakar, a seventeenth-century commentator, writes that Isaac's and Rebecca's attitude towards their two sons was a matter of proximity. Esau, he comments, "was not around (Heb. '*matzui*') his mother, so Rebecca didn't love him"[5] Jacob, on the other hand, stayed home in the tent with his mother, so she preferred his company. Esau accompanied the other men on the hunt, so Isaac learned to prefer him. Without over-psychoanalyzing, we might also imagine Isaac enjoying vicarious pleasure from his masculine, aggressive son Esau. Isaac, after all, was the passive, simple one compared to his brother Ishmael, a "wild man, his hand in everyone, everyone's hand in his."[6] Isaac may be responding the way any bookish, intellectual father responds to a more athletic son – with nostalgic admiration for everything he could not be.

But this explanation is disappointing, because surely parents should transcend their own self-images and appetites, and embrace their children's unique essential qualities. We would certainly expect even mediocre parents to overcome proximity. If Jacob's

---

2.   Genesis 25: 28.
3.   Ibid. 25: 27.
4.   Ibid.
5.   Kli Yakar to Genesis 25:28.
6.   Genesis 16:12.

not "*matzui*," shouldn't his father seek him out? If Esau went out to hunt rather than stay at home with his mother, shouldn't Rebecca find other ways to become close to him?

Rashi, an outstanding Biblical commentator of the Middle Ages, suggests a deeper motivation for Rebecca's closeness to Jacob. He claims that she was a prophetess, and therefore understood through the Holy Spirit that Jacob was the morally superior child. But if we transfer the story to our own terms (and certainly we're allowed to do that with the Bible), what does that really mean? Somehow Rebecca has a "feeling" that Jacob will be a better person than Esau. Even if it's a good feeling, a holy feeling, shouldn't a mother rise above her own inchoate feelings and learn to love all her children? No wonder Esau "howls a great and exceedingly bitter howl." It's the howl of every rejected child, every victim of imperfect parents who, intentionally or not, wound their children.

I can't claim that I howled when I read that my mother didn't really like me. I didn't even cry out. I simply put the diary away, and didn't look at it again until I cleaned out her nightstand, thirty days after she died of a fatal brain tumor. But her words wounded me, and if the hurt wasn't "exceedingly bitter," it has certainly lasted a long time. The fact is, both my father and mother fell into Rebecca and Isaac's flawed parent trap: at crucial times, neither transcended their own narrow world. My father gave in to his appetites with extra-marital affairs, which consequently wreaked havoc on our family life, damaging both his wife and his children. My mother, I believe, for a time at least, preferred Beth because she was "*matzui*" – she was proximate; she was around. Beth and my mother shared interests and sensibilities at a particularly vulnerable time in my mother's life, so she liked Beth, and not me (or my eleven-year-old brother, or my other sister who, at the time, was a baby). True, I only became fully aware of my mother's feelings when I read her secret thoughts, but, really, I knew. How can a son not know something like that? I'd known for years.

But maybe this is a good time to emphasize that I don't think of my father and mother as poor parents. On the contrary, I consider myself fortunate – even blessed – that I had such parents. On the most basic level, they provided for me – so that I was never hungry or lacking – but even more, I never felt unloved or unsupported. Until the day they each died, I received cogent, sympathetic, and loving advice about numerous topics, from parenting, to husbanding, to career. I never hung up the phone with either of them without feeling better about myself and my life than before I called. But still. The wound is there. The damn diary my sister showed me when I was ten years old.

Parents, of course, will always make mistakes, will never be able to stop their children from feeling pain, and will even sometimes be directly responsible for that pain. To me, that's part of the symbolism of the *brit milah* (circumcision) ceremony. The parent physically hands over the boy to the *mohel* (one who performs circumcision on a Jewish male as a religious rite) who then wounds him in a sensitive place. Right before my first son's circumcision, my wife asked the *mohel* if it would hurt. "Yes," he said, nodding sadly. Just my luck, I thought. I've got the world's only honest *mohel*. But it doesn't just hurt, it wounds. I remember thinking to myself, as we gave the *mohel* our baby, "Get used to it. Get used to creating pain for your child. It will happen again. And again." And I am not just talking about me, hurting my own child, but my son hurting his children, just like my parents wounded me. Perhaps that's why we wound the penis, the generative organ, to show that our wounding travels through the generations.

Jacob, Isaac's son, after all, famously hurt his own children by playing favorites with Joseph. Abraham wounded Isaac twice – with the first infant circumcision, and then the Binding of Isaac – before Isaac wounded his two sons. My parents hurt me, but then I've undoubtedly already wounded my children in astonishing and creative ways; different than my father, but possibly no less exceedingly bitter. No matter how loving, sympathetic, generous and responsible we become as parents, we make mistakes. We hurt our children. We wound them. So to say that my parents were like Isaac and Rebecca, to say that I suffered along with Esau, is only to say that they were human parents raising a human child.

Suffering with My Words

And yet I recently discovered a redemptive note to the Isaac-Esau scene, one that fits my life at least, if not every wounded child's. Isaac, in fact, does not leave Esau without a blessing. After repeated, plaintive proddings from Esau, Isaac says, "Your settlements shall glean the fat of the land and the dew of the sky above. You will live by your sword and serve your brother. But when you overcome, you shall break his yoke from your neck."[7] At first glance, this is certainly a lesser blessing than Jacob received. Specifically, Isaac tells Jacob that God will give him "the fat of the land" and "the dew of the sky,"[8] while Esau will only live among the bounty. Also, Isaac leaves out the phrase "bounteous grain and corn"[9] from Esau's blessing. Not to mention the fact that Isaac promises Jacob that he will rule over his brothers, while telling Esau that his brother will rule over him. So, from Esau's point of view, it's a disappointing blessing, even less than a consolation prize. Esau certainly receives the blessing in that spirit. He storms away, and resolves to kill Jacob.

Yet, for me, the key phrase is: "But when you overcome, you shall break his yoke from your neck." Actually, as so often occurs in the Torah, a single word reveals a profound truth. The Hebrew word I'm translating as "overcome" is *tarid*, whose root means, "rule oppressively," or, more colloquially, "come down hard on." Here, in its causative (*hiph'il*) form, it seems to mean the opposite: "when you un-rule" or, really, "overrule"; that is, when you remove the yoke from your neck. That would make the statement

7. Genesis 27:39–40.
8. Ibid. 27–28.
9. Ibid.

a meaningless tautology: "when you remove the yoke from your neck, you'll remove the yoke from your neck." But Rashi, comparing the word to another instance of it in Psalms, provides a fascinating insight. Defining *tarid*, he comments:

> It means "suffer." For example, "I suffer (Heb. *arid*) with my words" (Psalm 18). That is, when Israel violates the Torah, you will have an opening to suffer verbally, and bemoan the blessings which where taken from you.

Like many of Rashi's comments, we can understand it on many levels. On the national/political level, Rashi is claiming that when Israelites sin, our non-Jewish subjects – in this case the Edomites, Esau's descendants – are given the opportunity to articulate an authentic grievance to God, who will then respond by breaking the Israelite yoke, and setting the Edomites free. In this way, Rashi explains the history of the Israelite/Edomite conflict; the Edomites received their independence through a dialectical process which included Israelite sin and authentic Edomite prayer. Israelite sin gave the Edomites the very words they needed to express their national grievance.

But on a more personal level, Rashi is saying that there will come a time when Esau the person (as opposed to the Edomite nation) will finally be able to authentically articulate his unique sorrow, to talk about it, in the same way the Psalmists articulates his suffering through words. And when that happens, when Esau is able to describe his suffering in words, then he will break Jacob's yoke. He'll set himself free.

Which, of course, is exactly what I'm doing by writing this book. After more than thirty years, I'm describing the wounds. I'm suffering with my words. That's not a small thing for me. I hardly ever tell this story. I've only told my wife bits and pieces. My best friends don't know this story. My children will learn it for the first time if and when they read this. The fact is, this hasn't been an easy book to write for many obvious reasons, but perhaps most dramatically because it's exceedingly bitter for me to accuse two loving, well-intentioned, successful parents of wounding me. But, for me at least, Isaac's blessing is working. Writing about these experiences eases the pain (thirty years of distance also goes a long way). I'm freeing myself with my words, even if I haven't entirely removed the yoke from my neck.

There is, however, an even deeper dynamic at work. I received all the tools I've needed to reflect on this painful episode from my parents. Beyond the obvious – paying for my education, forcing me to do homework when I wanted to play basketball, the clichéd roles of Jewish parents everywhere – my parents specifically encouraged me to write. If it had been up to my mother, I would have pursued writing as a career, not the rabbinate. And my father, years after his death, remains my most important Torah teacher, my model on how to tease out meaning from the Torah using the nearly bottomless Jewish hermeneutic tradition. So, it's my parents' blessing which allows me to write about their sins, using the Torah as my most important lens.

In the Torah, when Jacob, many years after stealing Esau's blessing, wrestled with a mysterious being that turns out to be an angel, he emerged from the experience with both a wound and a blessing. The angel blesses him by giving him a new name – Israel – but also wounds him, bruising his thigh. He limps away. That's exactly what happened to me. I limped away with a blessing. My parents gave me a wound and a blessing – a blessing for me.

You Read My Diary?

Approximately twenty-three years after I first read my mother's diary, a congregant, who had also become a friend, approached me with her sad story. Her marriage was about to end. Her husband, she told me, had engaged in several extra-marital affairs. And now he was leaving her for a younger woman. She specifically asked for advice about her thirteen-year-old son. What should she tell him? How could she explain the divorce? Should she tell him about his philandering father? Naturally, the plight of the son moved me.

I couldn't help comparing him to my ten-year-old self suddenly faced with a flawed father.

Without thinking through the implications, I suggested to the woman that she speak with my mother, who happened to be in town, and who'd become quite friendly with this congregant. My mother, I told her, had shepherded four children through divorce, three out of four during the very heart of adolescence. She'd been an exemplary mother during these wretched times, never failing to offer love no matter what agony she was experiencing. The congregant liked the idea. I told her I'd check first with my mother.

"Why would she want to talk to me?" my mother asked, after I'd told her my friend's story. We were walking home from Shabbat services. It was a hot day, and I was sweating underneath my suit.

"There are so many similarities," I answered. "You were about her age. She has the kid. And there's the affairs."

She stopped walking. "What are you talking about?"

"Well, Dad had those affairs."

"How do you know about the affairs?" My mother normally had a gentle voice, but there was definitely an edge to her tone. She wasn't just asking, she was demanding.

I was momentarily speechless. "Well, the diary," I blurted out.

"The diary? What diary? How do you know about the diary?"

I was flabbergasted. She doesn't know. All these years, I thought, I've been wrong. "You left it out that time on the kitchen counter. Remember? The suicide note?"

"You read my diary?" my mother asked, but softly, not angrily. She seemed mostly concerned, and deeply puzzled. She turned away and stared off into space.

"Just once," I lied. "When I found the note. The suicide note."

She looked away for a long time, maybe five minutes. Then she started walking. She told me she'd be happy to talk to my friend.

A week later, Beth called me at work. "Did you tell Mom we'd read her diary?" This was the first time Beth had mentioned the diary to me in more than twenty years. In other words, this was the first time we'd spoken about it as adults. During the entire conversation, I felt as if we were discussing other individuals, strange, precocious, snotty kids who didn't hesitate before invading their mother's privacy. I found it hard to connect those unpleasant children with ourselves.

"It slipped out," I said. I told her the story. "It never occurred to me that Mom wouldn't know that we'd read the diary. I was sure she knew. But I was wrong. She didn't even know that we knew about the affairs."

"No kidding," she said. She'd just gotten off the phone with my mother. "She asked if I knew. And then she wanted to know how I found out. She asked me if I'd read her diary."

"What did you tell her?" I asked. Then I held my breath.

"I told her the truth. I told her we'd read it for years."

"Damn," I said.

"That's not what you told her."

"I told her I'd seen it once. Just that time I found the suicide note. Just once."

"But that wasn't true."

"No," I answered. "I lied. It wasn't true."

For weeks after that conversation, I expected an angry phone call from my mother. "Why did you lie?" she'd demand. Or, worse, "How could you read my diary, my private thoughts!" For weeks, in those days before caller ID, I hesitated in answering the phone. And when she did call, as she often would, just to say hello, or to check in with her grandchildren, my mouth went dry waiting for the inevitable. But it never happened. She never challenged my lie, never mentioned "Chronicles of a Broken Marriage."

Three years later, she died of a brain tumor, and I threw the diary into the trash.

But that's how I discovered that I'd been wrong all along. My mother never knew that she'd unleashed the awful secret on me at the tender age of ten. She didn't, as I'd once suspected, continue to write her awful thoughts, knowing that I would read them, even leaving them for me in the familiar place. My parents wounded me, but there was nothing intentional or cruelly perverse in their actions towards me. Like so many parental missteps, it was all carelessness and selfishness and appetite – a potent, tawdry combination which, nevertheless, doesn't even come close to reaching the level of downright evil. It was a wound, that's all; not a deathblow, not abuse, not premeditated murder. And it was more than balanced by years of blessing. A blessing and a wound: that's precisely what my parents bequeathed me. I limped away with a blessing. Or, I could say it this way. I limped away, but, in the fullness of time, their blessing for me set me free.

Chapter 2

WALKING ABOUT
IN THE CEMETERY

*To protect confidentiality,
some of the characters' names mentioned
in this chapter have been changed.*

Family Rabbi

The Rothstien funeral was not the first of my career, nor the second, but I'm pretty sure it was the third. I do know I was new at the game – a freshly minted Conservative rabbi, less than six weeks on the job as assistant rabbi at the Park Avenue Synagogue in Manhattan. I was leaning back in my overstuffed office chair early one morning, beginning, frankly, to doze, when I got the call.

"I've got one for you, Phil," Barney Fierburg barked at me over the phone. "David's away, so this one's yours." Barney, the chair of the search committee that brought me to the Park Avenue Synagogue, ran a swank Upper East Side funeral home. Two months earlier, after he'd informed me of the surprisingly low salary this wealthy synagogue was offering, he'd growled, "Don't worry. I'll throw some funerals your way. You'll do okay." I thought he was kidding. I even laughed, but Barney, ordinarily a jovial fellow – chubby and red-faced, he looked more like a deli-man than an undertaker – didn't crack a smile. He wasn't kidding. I made a lot of money performing funerals my first two years at Park Avenue, thanks to Barney "throwing them my way."

The first one he threw at me was Marcello Rothstien. He ticked off the facts. "58 years old. Rich businessman. Importer. Born in Cuba. Two grown kids, a wife and a sister. Lived on 88th and Madison."

"Hmm," I responded, trying to shake off my drowsiness. With my boss Rabbi David Lincoln away, I had to get up every morning at 5:30, so I could cover the morning service. I wasn't used to getting up that early.

"Call over there now, Phil," Barney instructed. "I told them they'd hear from you."

"Uh, sure, Barney," I said, quickly taking down the information. One detail, of course, stuck out. "Uh, Barney, did you say 58 years old?"

He grunted. "Younger than me, as it happens."

"Heart attack?"

"Uh, not exactly."

"Well?"

"Now, listen, the police aren't exactly sure."

"What is it, Barney, suicide?"

"No, more like murder."

That woke me up.

"They found him behind his apartment building with a knife in his back. Probably wasn't an accident. But listen, I don't want to report rumors. Just remember your job. You go over there, shake hands with the boys, calm down the sister who seems a little hysterical, say some nice words, and set up the service. Don't worry; you get paid no matter how he died."

And so do you, I thought. "Yeah, but Barney –"

"Look, I'm not a cop. I don't know what happened. But let's just say he may have been importing some of the wrong stuff. And selling it to the wrong people. It's been known to happen, even to Jews. Listen, if you really want to know, you should read today's *Daily News*. It's only on the front page."

I tried to pry out more information, but Barney was a busy man, with more funerals to take care of. I called the Rothstien apartment, spoke briefly to Ben, the older son, and made an appointment to visit the family that day.

On the walk over to 88th Street, I stopped at a newsstand to look at the *Daily News*. MILLIONAIRE MOB BOSS SLAIN BEHIND HOUSE screamed the full page headline (not, actually, an over-dramatic response for the *Daily News*). The subhead revealed a detail Barney had chosen to leave out. CHIEF SUSPECT: SPURNED WIFE.

I bought the newspaper and read about Marcello Rothstien, the "Millionaire Mob Boss." According to unnamed sources (the cops, the Justice Department, "family sources"), Rothstien was suspected of running his own drug mini-empire, importing opium from independent farms in South America. Despite his respectable Madison Avenue address, sophisticated social connections, and Ivy League sons, Rothstien had spent several years behind bars, both in the United States and Mexico, mostly for drug dealing, but also for battery, attempted homicide, and drunk driving. In short, he was a violent gangster who had ended his tawdry life in an alleyway with a knife sticking out of his back.

Surprisingly, none of the sources thought his criminal associates had anything to do with his death. A senior source explained that it wasn't a "hit." Backstabbings in alleyways were not the way drug lords did business. Too messy and unreliable. Besides, despite his wealth and success, Rothstien was not really a major player. He wasn't, in other words, important enough to murder. The "spurned wife," on the other hand, she had a motive. Police sources reported that just two weeks earlier, Rothstien had kicked her out of the house after twenty-five years of marriage, and then announced to his family that he was planning on marrying a twenty-five-year-old model (whose picture graced most of page 6 of the newspaper. She was climbing into a car, smiling at the camera). Family sources claimed to have overheard the enraged wife Judith threaten to kill Rothstien several times. They even reported seeing her grab a kitchen knife and wave it around her head, while swearing at her husband in Spanish.

As I made my way to the Rothstien residence, I somehow imagined Judith answering the door, bloody knife in hand. But it was Ben, the older son, a tall, dark, clean-cut young man in his early twenties who ushered me into the spacious, elegant apartment. He introduced me to his younger brother Joseph and his aunt Ida. I looked around the living room and glanced into the kitchen, but the chief suspect was nowhere in sight.

An elaborate spread of cheeses, cold cuts, caviar, sour cream, smoked fish, pickles, tomatoes, radishes, and olives covered the huge, shiny, oak dining room table. A collection of china dolls, thirty or forty of varying sizes, adorned the mantle; Persian rugs decorated the hardwood floors. Like many of the Upper East Side homes I had visited in the previous weeks, the apartment was large, and expensively decorated. Both Ben and Joseph wore suits. Ida sported a mid-length black skirt and a white blouse. The whole scene gave me the impression of old, Park Avenue, money, even though I now understood that it was new, drug money, from Colombia. Ben and Joseph, with their courtly manners and reserved, soft-spoken grief, added to the impression of gentility. It was difficult to imagine that this had been the home of a crook – an only mildly successful one at that.

I shook hands all around and offered my condolences. We sat on a white sofa. After a few moments of awkward silence, I asked about the deceased. In response, Ida looked to Joseph, who stared at Ben, who studied the Persian rug. Inwardly, I berated myself. What can they possibly say about their father and brother? He had sold drugs for a living, spent time in prison, and maybe even killed people. He had knifed a friend once during an argument. Kicked out his wife – Ben and Joseph's mother – and picked up with a blond model. He was, in other words, a monster.

"He was a saint," Ben told me, suddenly looking me right in the eye, as if daring me to contradict him.

"Pardon me?" I asked. I was sure I had misheard.

"A saint," Ida agreed, wiping away tears I hadn't noticed until that moment. "And generous! The most generous man you'd ever meet. Gave away money like candy."

"Yes, and compassionate," Joseph piped in. "Unbelievably compassionate. You know the homeless? Those people who sleep on the street?"

I nodded, indicating that I knew what "homeless" meant.

"They made him cry. He would cry his eyes out every time we took a walk. You never met a man so compassionate."

His brother nodded. "Family always came first," he said. "Always family. That was his most important value. Whenever we had a problem, if we needed advice or direction, he was always there for us. Remember when I almost dropped out of law school? You see, rabbi, I was actually considering going to rabbinical school. Eventually, he talked me out of it, but he made it clear he would support me, no matter what, no matter what path I chose in life. Even if I ended up a bum."

Or a rabbi, I was tempted to add. Or a drug-dealer.

"Did you know he prayed?" Ida continued. She slowly rotated her head, staring into each of our eyes, as if telling a story around a campfire. "He did! He prayed every day. He didn't use a prayerbook, rabbi, he didn't even know Hebrew. But he *talked* to God. That's why he was so firm, and satisfied, and serene, and quiet. Because he prayed. He told me that was his secret. It's not that he was a religious man, rabbi, I don't want to mislead you. He had, well we all know his difficulties, his, uh, mistakes. He was no Orthodox Jew, that's for sure. But he had a way about him. He was *spiritual*. That's really the word. He was a spiritual man."

She burst into tears. Ben offered a handkerchief, which she took, blew loudly, and then calmed herself, taking deep breaths. But then she broke down altogether, weeping uncontrollably. I reached over to comfort her.

"That *bitch* killed him," she spit out, almost at the exact moment my hand reached her shoulder. I drew it back quickly. She blew her nose again into the handkerchief, and in a determined, anguished voice, proclaimed, "Judith killed him! The bitch! She stabbed him! I can prove it!"

"Aunt Ida!" Ben quickly interrupted. "We agreed! We were not going to do this!"

"I know, Ben, but I can't help it. The rabbi should know. He has a *right* to know!"

"No," Joseph said. "This is not the time. We agreed!"

"Rabbi Graubart," Ben turned to me. "Forgive us. We didn't want to involve you in our family feud. It's a complicated story. You see, my parents–"

"That bitch killed him, Ben!"

"This is not the time!" Ben stated firmly, taking control. He stared down his aunt, then whispered a sentence in Spanish. Ida answered back, and for the next five minutes the three bereaved family members conducted an animated Spanish conversation, with dramatic hand gestures, harsh gutturals, screams, whispers, and tears. Since they were all fluent English speakers, their clear intent was to exclude me. And it worked. Even though I'd taken three years of high school Spanish, the only word I recognized was *muerte*.

"Rabbi Graubart," Ben said finally, "I'd be happy to explain."

"Oh, there's no need," I said, in fact sort of wishing that he wouldn't.

"My parents were separated," he said.

"Ah!" I answered, as if that explained everything, the fighting, the crying, the murder.

"They were not living together as husband and wife."

"I see," I said.

"Bitch." I heard Ida mutter, under her breath.

I stayed for another hour, chatting pleasantly with the boys about their father's hobbies (always, I've found, a safe topic, even in the most dysfunctional families). It turned out that in addition to prayer, Marcello enjoyed mountain climbing and scuba diving. I scribbled down some notes, thinking that crafting these facts into a eulogy would be quite a challenge. I spoke about the funeral service, explaining every ritual that we would perform the following day. Ida said nothing the entire hour, but she did pay careful attention, particularly as I explained the ritual of *kri'ah*, tearing one's clothing as a gesture of grief.

We set a time to meet the next day, and I got up to leave. Ida instantly grabbed my by the arm and led me to the door. The boys said their goodbyes, and waved. Ida reached up with two hands, grabbed my head, and pulled my ear to her mouth. "She killed him," she hissed, and I felt her hot breath shoot up my eardrum. "She killed him. And he was a *saint*."

On my way home, I stopped at a newsstand and noticed Rothstien's picture, this time on the cover of the *Post*. "THE WIFE DID IT!" the headline screamed. "High School Sweetheart Knifed Millionaire Mob Boss Behind Building." I bought the paper.

The *Post* painted an even more alarming picture of Rothstien than the *Daily News*. This article spoke of paternity suits. The reporter interviewed several anonymous mistresses who also spoke of Rothstien's "fiery" temper, his serial philandering, his cocaine use, his cruel manner toward his wife. Neighbors spoke of wild parties, the sounds of gunshots, and murderous, screaming arguments in Spanish. Unnamed police and district attorney sources were unanimous. "We're looking at the wife." "It looks like the wife did it." "This is no mob hit." "We'll have an arrest, soon." "She did it."

I met Judith Rothstien the next day. She was the first person to greet me as I pushed through the heavy side doors at the 83rd Street entrance to Fierburg's Funeral Home. "Robert," she called out, as I headed to the elevator. That's not my name, so I didn't think to look up. But she grabbed my arm just as the doors were opening, and slipped in beside me. "Robert?" she asked.

I told her my name was Philip.

"That's not what the newspaper says."

"The newspaper?"

She took out a copy of that day's *Daily News* and opened to the second page. I saw a picture of myself rushing out of Rothstien's apartment building, looking oddly guilty. I took the paper and read a short article recounting the seamy details of the life and death of Marcello Rothstien. It reviewed the police's interest in "the scorned wife, Mrs. Judith Rothstien." The final paragraph noted that "the family rabbi, Rabbi Robert Graubart, would be officiating at the prestigious Fierburg Funeral Home on the Upper East Side of Manhattan."

I looked at the scorned wife. Though noticeably worn down, with small bags under her eyes, leaky eye make-up, and a large collection of worry creases across her forehead, she still struck an attractive pose. She was tall, slim, with high cheekbones, pure black hair, and a flawless complexion. She could have passed for thirty, though I knew from the newspapers that she couldn't be younger than forty-five. She wore a shiny, low-cut black gown, with black high heels – more appropriate, I thought, for the academy awards than her husband's funeral. Her overall appearance was dazzling. It was hard to take my eyes off of her, and I realized, after a few moments, that I was staring.

"I recognized your picture," she told me, taking the newspaper away from me. "But they must have gotten your name wrong. Are you sure it isn't Robert?"

I was wondering how to best answer that one when the elevator door opened, and we both stepped out into the wide hallway. I took it as a chance for a getaway. I muttered "excuse me," and rushed into one of the tiny, windowless offices Barney provided for clergy. I turned on the light in the cell-like room, and was about to breathe a sigh of relief, when, to my astonishment, I saw Mrs. Rothstien standing next to me, a vacant, lost expression on her face, her gown brushing against my suit. I quickly squeezed past her, and sat behind the flimsy white desk with the chipped paint. Clumsily, I gestured at a folding chair leaning against the wall. Judith unfolded the chair, fell into it, then threw the top half of her body halfway across the desk, laying her head on her arms. She lay still for several seconds, her long black hair covering every inch of the desk. I assumed she was crying, though she wasn't making any noise.

I didn't know what to do. She was acting genuinely bereaved, which could have convinced me, despite the many anonymous sources, that she wasn't the killer after all. On the other hand, even the real killer can display grief, especially if the person she killed had been her husband of twenty-five years. It seemed proper that I should comfort her, assuming she hadn't fallen asleep on the desk. But was it right to offer condolences to someone whose misery was caused by her own act of murder? It seems unnecessary to say that this wasn't the type of thing we learned about in rabbinical school.

Finally, she looked up. Several tiny, ball-bearing shaped tears rolled down her cheeks. I'd never seen tears so round.

"Thank you," she said, exhaling slowly. "Thank you."

She must have seen the confused look on my face – what on Earth was she thanking me for? – because she added, "for letting me cry on your desk."

"You're welcome," I said cautiously, careful not to give her the impression that she should feel free to do it again.

"Rabbi Graubart," she said. "Philip. Do you think the dead live on? After they die?"

I asked her to repeat the question. She did.

Now, as it happens, I had strong opinions on the subject, and I still do. Complicated opinions, but strong. But as a young rabbi, I had a bad habit of responding to questions with the answers I thought the questioners wanted to hear. So I always paused before answering, not to come up with the right answer, but with the answer I thought would work best. So I paused and studied the wife, who may also have been the killer. Then I told her that certainly the dead live on in our memories.

"No, no, I don't mean any of that," she said quickly. "I don't mean *symbolically*. I mean really live. Can the dead communicate with the living?" I watched her brush the hair out of her eyes. "You see," she said, "I've spoken to my husband. Several times, in fact."

"What does he say?" I blurted out. To this day, I'm not sure why I asked such a ridiculous question, other than I was truly curious. What does a victim say to his killer? Or maybe I was trying to get her to confess. To solve the Rothstien murder right there and then in the prestigious Fierburg Funeral Home.

"It doesn't matter what he said, Philip," Judith answered sharply. "That's hardly the point, is it? Anyway, isn't that getting a little personal? I just want to know from you, as a rabbi. You are a rabbi aren't you?"

I nodded.

"Okay, then. In your opinion, can dead people talk to living people?"

I told her the truth. I said that I believed it could happen. I told her that it's certainly something the Jewish tradition accepts as a possibility.

"A possibility," she said. Another ball-bearing tear leaked from her eyes. "Okay, so tell me this. Aren't the dead supposed to get punished for all the rotten things they did on Earth? Isn't there some kind of retribution? Doesn't Judaism teach something about horrible punishments?"

"Horrible?" I said. "I'm not so sure about horrible; though, I guess it would depend on the sins."

"I'm talking about the next world, Philip. I think you know what I mean. Fire. And uh, I don't know, a pit. And whips and snakes. You *know*," she said, accusingly, as if I were holding back on her.

I was about to answer when the door swung open. Benjamin Rothstien, the older son, stepped in, looking sad and strong, dignified, and tall – taller than I remembered from the previous night. He stared down at Judith.

"Mother," he said evenly.

She rose from her chair, stumbling a bit before finding her footing. It was only then I realized that she was probably drunk, or stoned. She reached out to grab Benjamin's wrist, then fell into his arms. Watching her smooth profile, I noticed three ball-bearing tears float down her cheek.

With pictures of fiery whips and snakes floating through my mind, I followed mother and son into the sanctuary. The first thing I noticed when I stepped up to the lectern was four tall men in identical blue blazers, with white shirts, black ties, and dark glasses, each standing in one of the four corners of the room. Bodyguards, I figured, or maybe cops, or even FBI agents. I also saw that the entire third row was filled with jeans-clad, unkempt young men and women, all scribbling on notepads, or tapping into laptops. Obviously reporters. The rest of the hall overflowed with expensively-dressed, impeccably-groomed mourners; none, in my mind, resembling drug-lords or gangsters. But what did I know? The Rothstien family sat in the front row. Missing, as far as I could tell was the model – the new fiancée. But Judith pressed herself firmly against Benjamin, holding his hand tightly in her lap. At her right, almost touching her elbow, was her chief accuser, Aunt Ida, who alternated between fits of weeping, and deadly stares directed at her former sister-in-law.

In my eulogy, I talked about Rothstien's love of prayer. I called him an excellent father, and a spiritual person. I hinted that it wasn't our place to judge him, particularly not at this time. I talked about forgiveness. It was my first and only eulogy to be commented on by the New York tabloids. The *Post* referred to it as "moving and heartfelt." Or something to that effect.

Next came a scene straight out of "A Hard Day's Night." As soon as I pronounced the service over, the reporters jumped out of their seats and rushed to the Rothstien limousine. Barney grabbed my arm, and whisked me, along with the family, into his office. It turned out he'd set up a decoy limo, complete with actors, dressed up to impersonate the Rothstien family. The reporters who fall for it, Barney told me, will be headed on a wild goose chase toward New Jersey.

We sat silently in Barney's office, waiting for the crowd to thin out. No one said a word, but Ida kept a steady stare on Judith. Finally, we snuck out the side door. Unfortunately, not all the reporters were fooled by the fake limo (apparently, it's on old ruse), so they jumped at us as soon as we emerged. But Barney had another trick up his sleeve. He sent out a young, pretty, blond actress with sunglasses, and she ambled slowly toward another of his limousines. Barney whispered to me that she's the spitting image of Marcello Rothstien's fiancée. Most of the remaining reporters and photographers ran after the blonde; even more hustled her way when she stopped for a moment, looking eager to talk. Meanwhile, Barney tossed each of us into our actual limo, and we pealed out toward the FDR Drive.

We pulled into the cemetery gate, only to encounter another small hoard of indefatigable paparazzi, too clever for Barney's tricks. Flashbulbs exploded in my face; my eyes swam with black dots. Our driver, a muscular, craggy-faced old man who looked like he could easily have gotten a job with one of Rothstien's colleagues, bolted out of the car, swearing like a sailor, and shook his fists at the reporters. Barney whipped out his cellphone (rare in those days, but, of course Barney needed one), and called the cops. They arrived within minutes, lights flashing, and quickly shooed away the mad pack. The family and I climbed slowly out of the car, our eyes still smarting. I took a breath, shielded my eyes from the sun, and looked around. We were the only ones left. No reporters, no crowd of grieving mourners. Just the family and myself.

At the gravesite, I stumbled through the memorial prayers. I found myself rushing. For some reason, I couldn't get the image of Judith's ball-bearing tears out of my mind. I also remembered her description of snakes and fiery whips, and visits from Rothstien. In an absurd moment, as I pronounced his Hebrew name, I wondered if he would visit me, and ask me about Judith. Get a grip! I told myself, and slowed down.

At the end of the prayer, I helped each of the Rothstiens – the boys, Aunt Ida, and Judith – take a shovelful of dirt and pitch it into the open grave. I grabbed a handful myself and tossed it onto the coffin. No one in the family got through the mourner's *kaddish* (a Jewish prayer recited by mourners at public services after the death of a close relative) without crying. The chief suspect's round tears splashed on to the grave with a plunking sound, like raindrops falling on a tin roof. I chanted the final prayer, then guided the family back to the limousine.

I was about to step into Barney's car – he was going to take me home separately from the Rothstiens – when I felt a cold hand on my arm. I froze and thought of Rothstien and fiery whips. But it was just Ida. She stood on her toes and leaned into my ear. "She killed him," she hissed in a voice that would have been audible if I'd been standing 100 feet away. It was a hateful, poisonous voice, thin but remarkable for its malignant power. I looked up and saw Judith, still arm in arm with both sons, grimace, and then turn away. There's no doubt she heard the accusation; we all heard it, plain as day. Ben ran up to me and apologized for his aunt's outburst. "Aunt Ida," he said, "this is *not* the time!"

"But she *killed* him," she said, right out loud, now not even bothering to whisper. "You know it. Joseph knows it." She turned towards me again. "It's her, Rabbi Graubart. That bitch." She pointed at her former sister-in-law like a prosecutor gesturing at the accused in front of a jury. "She killed my brother."

"Enough!" Ben said, and grabbed her, wrestling her into the limo.

"But he should *know!*" Ida protested, struggling. "The rabbi, at least, should know. Who else should know, if *not* the rabbi?"

Dumbstruck, I stared at the wrestling match between Ben and Ida, and watched Ben finally shove his aunt into the back seat of the car. As the door slammed shut, I noticed Judith glaring at Ida, and Ida glowering right back. Both wore faces of total fury, murderous faces, reflecting a hatred so dreadful and electric, it could only be shared by the most intimate of companions.

Whodunit

I've written two fictionalized accounts of the Rothstien incident: a published short story, and an (as yet) unpublished novel. Clearly, it was an important moment in my life, and I've felt compelled to use the arduous process of narrative twice (now, three times) as a vehicle to work through my feelings. In the two fictionalized versions, the rabbi (me!) receives a mysterious packet of letters shortly after the funeral. In the unpublished novel, an imagined Rothstien daughter (an old girlfriend – fictional) drops them off for me for her own nefarious and byzantine purposes. In the short story, the letters just appear out of nowhere, on my desk. In both cases, they would become important clues as to who really murdered Rothstien. As a fiction writer, I couldn't resist adding a touch of whodunit suspense to my work. And who could blame me? At the time of the funeral, Rothstien's murder really was a mystery, though the tabloid press kept quoting sources insisting that Judith did it.

But here's what really happened. Judith *wasn't* the killer. Two days after the burial, I read that the police arrested a Colombian man for the murder. After all the allegations and incriminations against Judith, it did in fact turn out to be a drug hit. Even a small-timer like Rothstien couldn't get away with cutting in on the wrong territory. Rothstien, as far as I know, never again appeared in the newspaper. His fifteen minutes of fame ended with that last article. Mine, of course, was much shorter; I was mentioned just a few times in the press – Rabbi Robert Graubart, "family rabbi."

As for the packet of letters, they were real; I did receive them; they appeared on my desk. But there were only two, and there was no mystery involved. Judith sent them to me, and my secretary placed them neatly on my desk, resisting the urge to open and read them. One was a brief thank-you note, apologizing for showing up stoned to the funeral. She enclosed a check for $500 in that envelope, even though Barney had already paid me. In the much longer second letter, she described for me, in great detail, what it was like to be married to the likes of Marcello Rothstien. It was, she wrote, a living hell, a nightmare of drug addiction, violent out-bursts, and, of course, serial infidelities. She described for me, just as an example, one night when Rothstien arrived home at two in the morning, bombed out on cocaine, and reeking from the odors of another woman. Judith, no softy, railed and swore at him for ten straight minutes, working herself into such a lather that she grabbed a vase and threatened to beat him over the head with it. Rothstien, partly in self-defense, but partly also out of sheer aggressive, meanness, slapped Judith hard across the face, sending the expensive vase flying into the wall, caroming onto the floor and shattering into hundreds of tiny pieces. Judith responded by punching Rothstien in the stomach. That ignited a genuine brawl – a Three-Stooges style festival of hitting, kicking, biting, and punching, where both fighters ended up wounded, requiring emergency medical attention. Oddly, Judith wrote, they shared a cab to the emergency room, and afterwards back home.

The hate-filled, violent, last five years of her marriage confounded Judith, because she still retained vivid, poignant memories of a time when she adored Marcello, when she found him not only gentle and loving, but charming, passionate, and charismatic. She also admitted that he was always a good father to Ben and Joseph, and a good brother to Ida. Their intense expressions of grief ("He was a saint!") had not been, as I had in fact suspected, faked, or even exaggerated. It's possible, Judith told me, that Ida didn't even realize that her brother had been a drug dealer and a murderer. She wasn't even sure how much her sons knew. According to Judith, Rothstien had been a popular guy, charitable, funny, and gregarious, with many sincere friends and admirers. The crowd at the funeral wasn't just made up of reporters, bodyguards, and federal agents. He was well-liked, and he would be missed. In other words, Rothstien was a complicated figure, with powerful, conflicting sides to his personality. He was loving and generous, but also brutal, violent, and even, sometimes, downright evil.

It was difficult, Judith wrote me, to imagine a man as viciously alive as Rothstien, decomposing in a grave. Which was why, she presumed, she continued to dream, nearly every night, that he visited her. She understood that these were just dreams, not actual visitations. When not under the influence of alcohol and pills, she was a fairly rational woman. But she'd never experienced dreams this vivid; dreams where, upon waking, she could recall odors of sweat, and fresh blood; or remember the various shades of pink in the flesh of Rothstien's flogged back. In each of these dreams, Rothstien would first describe a punishment he received in hell, and then, using some infernal video device, he would show Judith actual scenes of his degradations. So she watched her ex-husband suffer through floggings and burnings; heard his screams; smelled his burnt flesh. Then she would wake up in a panic.

It seems so real, she wrote to me. I couldn't possibly imagine the revoltingly *real* texture of these dreams. She knew Rothstien was dead; she wasn't insane. But, having lived through these ghastly nightmares, Judith no longer completely trusted the boundary between life and death. He's leaking through, she wrote me. She wrote it again. He's leaking through.

In her final paragraph, she wondered if she could come and see me, and perhaps continue the discussion we'd begun about Judaism and the afterlife. She wanted to discuss the subject with me in greater depth, and hear my opinions about this world and the next. She left me a phone number and a post office box address. She hoped we could stay in touch.

I, to say the least, wasn't crazy about the idea. Yes, she had been cleared of the murder, but she still didn't strike me as someone I necessarily wanted to "stay in touch" with, as if we were old friends. Nevertheless, I called her. I was, after all, "the family rabbi." But the line had been disconnected, and there was no information about a new number. I wrote to her post office box, but the letter was returned a week later, with no forwarding address. I called the Rothstien house twice and left messages for Ben but he never returned my calls. I thought of looking up Ida, but the memory of her bitter, vengeful accusations chilled me. So I gave up. I was a rabbi, not a detective. It wasn't my job to track down Judith Rothstien. I never saw her again, though I did check the tabloids for several months, just to see if her name would pop up. It never did.

I would probably remember the entire episode merely as darkly humorous – a weird, funny tale I could tell colleagues and friends, a comedy, not a tragedy or a ghost story – if it weren't for my own dreams about Marcello Rothstien. They started, strangely enough, the day after the funeral, in other words *before* Judith wrote to me about her own nightmares. In my first one, Rothstien complained that I'd screwed up the burial. He appeared in my office in a business suit, pounded his fist on my desk, and insisted that I'd forgotten about *kri'ah* – ceremonially tearing a piece of clothing, often a black ribbon. He also yelled at me for not giving the mourners a chance to toss dirt into the grave. Now, in reality, I had done both these things, the *kri'ah* and the dirt, but, in my dream, I agreed that I had, in fact, forgotten both of them. I was deeply ashamed, and also vaguely worried. Finally, Rothstien chewed me out because I'd forgotten to pour two gallons of water in the coffin. Even in my dream state, that one puzzled me. I'd never heard of such a custom. In any case, because of these blunders ("rookie mistakes" he called them), Rothstien was stuck in this world. He'd have to hang around, he explained, until I either cut Judith's dress with a knife, or, better yet, brought his killer to justice. The following night, the night before, in real life, I read Judith's letter. Rothstien, in this equally vivid dream, repeated his accusations and instructions, but this time waved a knife at me, and told me to use it either to cut Judith's dress, or to kill his killer. In the dream, Rothstien spoke Spanish, but, somehow, I understood everything he said.

"He's leaking through." That's what Judith wrote. You're telling me, I thought. She had stopped trusting the border between life and death. I read those words with a chill. I wasn't so sure of the border myself. Rothstien kept leaking through for the next several weeks, though the dreams gradually lost their vividness. After a month, I'd just wake up occasionally in the middle of a night with the uneasy impression that I'd screwed up somehow with Rothstien's burial. Even though I distinctly remembered performing *kri'ah* and urging the mourners to toss in the first shovels of dirt, and I knew the water accusation was a bit of dreamy nonsense, I'd still wake up feeling as if I'd made some serious rookie mistakes. The dreams went away, but the idea of Rothstien leaking through the Divide on account of my mistakes took a little longer to fade.

I understood, to the extent we can understand anything as complex as our own dreams, what was happening in my mind. Deep down, I felt guilty about my behavior during the affair. I hadn't really offered any comfort to the two grieving sons, no genuine words of wisdom, no practical advice. I'd avoided the sister. I'd behaved cruelly to Judith, assuming, wrongly, that she was the killer. I reacted to her authentic torment with my own fear and loathing. I made rookie mistakes. In response, my guilt invaded my subconscious in the form of a knife-wielding Marcello Rothstien, berating me for ritual infractions. In years to come, similar feelings of guilt would emerge after virtually every funeral. I'd fret over whether I was sufficiently comforting to the mourners, or eloquent enough at the eulogy, but also whether I made any mistakes. Did I forget any rituals? Or mispronounce the name of the deceased? Or skip an essential prayer? In moments of whimsy, I'd even ask myself: did my mistakes hinder the person's journey to heaven? Would the deceased, on account of my mistakes, leak through?

Rothstien's insistence, in my dreams, that I find his killer may have symbolized my feeling of having left something unfinished, by not seriously following through with the grieving family after the service. The Rothstiens weren't members of my congregation. I wasn't, despite the *Post*'s assertion, the "family rabbi," so I didn't try very hard afterwards, particularly because of the disturbing circumstances. But I did feel guilty, so my unconscious conjured up Rothstien, in the form of vivid nightmares, to remind me that I'd left something undone. Now, twenty years later, I always follow through diligently with the family of the deceased, often for years, no matter how unpleasant the circumstances, and, of course, regardless of whether the family does or does not belong to my synagogue. So Rothstien's ghost taught me something.

Deadman

But there's likely a more prosaic, less didactic, explanation for my dreams about Rothstien. When I was a kid, I was a great fan of the "Deadman" comic books, where the hero, a murdered "dead man," is stuck in limbo until he can bring his killer to justice. From age eight to fifteen, I was an avid comic-book collector, and the relatively obscure "Deadman" was my favorite character. As it happens, Marcello Rothstien bore a slight physical resemblance to the comic-book hero. So, given the other circumstances, I probably dreamt about finding the killer because Rothstien reminded me of Deadman.

Which brings up another possible reason why Marcello Rothstien haunted my dreams, and why the incident still disturbs me. I've always been obsessed with the question of what happens after we die. One of my earliest memories, at age four, is my sister Beth first explaining to me that ghosts were dead people who hadn't yet gone to heaven. Immediately after that conversation, I became convinced that our house was haunted. For a long time, possibly longer than a year, I couldn't fall asleep unless I closed my closet door tightly and stuffed some pillows under my bed and under the bed of my brother, in order to imprison the ghosts. As this particular delusion faded over time, I still remained intensely curious about the border between life and death. I peppered my father, a rabbi, with questions about the afterlife. Where is heaven? What happens there? Who gets to go? Can the folks in heaven communicate with the living? He put me off at first, much in the same way I avoided Mrs. Rothstien, by explaining how people achieve immortality through the legacies they leave behind, and the memories they create. But I was a tenacious investigator, and these abstract ideas didn't satisfy me at all, just as they hadn't satisfied Judith. Finally, with agitation in his voice, he blurted out: "We go with God!" That shut me up for a while, but

I remained convinced, far more I think than most children are past the age of nine or ten, that some intermediate stage existed between life and oblivion. In other words, up until the age of ten or eleven, I believed in ghosts. Truth be told, I'm not sure I have ever completely abandoned that belief. I enjoyed the "Deadman" comic books not just for the fantastic plots, but because, in some way, the premise rang true. Dead people with unfinished business couldn't make it to heaven. It made sense to me. They stayed here stuck, on our side of the border. Or, another way of putting it: they leaked through.

As a Conservative rabbinical student, a sophisticated reader of both theology and religious anthropology, I retained stubbornly concrete ideas about the afterlife. After we die, I believed, our immortal souls are first punished for the evil we commit on Earth, and then spend eternity in Heaven, with God. I'm not entirely sure how I acquired this shockingly traditional belief. Partly, I suppose, because my father taught it to me at an impressionable age, and partly because it's just something I've somehow always known to be true. In practical rabbinics classes, I'd listen to homiletics professors urge us to offer such words of comfort as, "there's no greater immortality than memory" – the very same words I first tried to pawn off on Mrs. Rothstien – and a voice inside of me would protest, "How lame! How can you quantify a term like immortality? What's the *second* greatest type of immortality? What's the worst? The greatest form of immortality is immortality itself!" Nevertheless, I sat and absorbed the reigning religious rationalism about death – the flight to abstraction and metaphor – and graduated rabbinical school armed with my own vocabulary of lame apologetics.

With her morbid questions, her rude rejection of my apologetics, and her insistence on describing in graphic detail her own theories about the afterlife, murder suspect Judith Rothstien had awakened my earlier beliefs and obsessions. With her probing, her oddly shaped tears, her story, and later her searing letters, she sent Marcello Rothstien into my dreams, where he stayed for a month, and where he pops up again every once in awhile, reminding me of a world in between life and death, a limbo, a purgatory inhabited by himself, Deadman, other murder victims, and assorted ghosts and goblins.

Upon Reflection

Rabbi Hiyya and Rabbi Jonathan were once walking about in a cemetery, and the blue fringes of Rabbi Jonathan were trailing on the ground.

> *Said Rabbi Hiyya to him, "Lift them up, so that they [the dead] should not say, 'Tomorrow they are coming here to join us, and now they mock us!'"*
> *He said to him, "But do they know?"*

> – Talmud, B. Berachot 18A

Do They Know?

Whenever I teach about Judaism's approach to death and dying, someone invariably raises their hand and comments with some indignation, "I thought Jews didn't believe in the afterlife!" Usually, at that point, heads nod all around, and the crowd begins to suspect that their teacher isn't representing authentic Judaism; that he may, in fact, be making the whole thing up, quotes and all. Somehow, a great percentage of American Jews, possibly a majority, have gotten the impression that Judaism denies the notion of life after death. But this isn't true. Yes, the Hebrew Bible teaches almost nothing about a world beyond this life. But post-biblical Jewish sources contain a rich and varied literature describing the afterlife.

A long passage in the Talmud (*Berachot* 18A), for example, presents a debate not on whether or not there's life after death (that's assumed), but on how much the inhabitants of the afterlife know about what's happening on our side of the border. There's some anxiety here, some ambivalence. When Rabbi Jonathan asks, "Do they know?" on the one hand, he's simply asking, out of curiosity. On the other hand, he's worried. Will we hurt their feelings if we don't lift our fringes? If so, can we also, unknowingly, hurt their feelings in other ways? Do they resent us because we can wear fringes, and they can't? Are they, in other words, jealous of our being alive? Are they ghosts? Will they hurt us?

His simple question – "Do they know?" – initiates the dueling anxieties that fuel what's certainly the Talmud's most bizarre debate. Both the rabbinic participants in the debate, and later readers (like me), come to the issue with mixed feelings. On the one hand, we're worried that the deceased don't "know." Despite the reassurances of hundreds of Talmudic and post-Talmudic texts, we can't erase the fear that death represents the total cessation of consciousness, of knowing. On the other hand, we're afraid that they do know, because that would imply the existence of an unseen world where ghosts cross over to our side of the border and spy on us, or worse. We face a natural conflict when thinking about death. We don't want it to be the end; we want to retain our contact with our world, our previous sense of being alive. But we don't want those who've died already to have *too* much contact with us. We're all at least a little afraid of ghosts.

The Talmudic discussion begins with the opposing rabbis offering verses from the Bible that either prove or disprove the proposition that the dead "know." But they can't seem to draw any conclusion from the competing texts. In fact, for this debate, Scripture is incompetent in deciding the issue. For believing Jews, the Biblical text creates an anxiety feedback loop. On the one hand, when read literally, the Hebrew Bible barely mentions the afterlife. So studying the Bible contextually provokes a fear of death. We learn, straight from the text, that our bodies smolder in the grave. Consciousness ends. This idea is so distressing that with the help of post-Biblical commentaries (like the Talmud), we look again at the Biblical verses and, lo and behold, after much creative, deep study, we discover that the Torah of Moses does indeed discuss the afterlife in great detail, though not, of course, explicitly. For example, Talmudic rabbis creatively "prove" the existence of an afterlife based on what is written in Numbers 18:28 and Exodus 6:4 (see Talmud, B. *Sanhedrin* 90B, for this and several other examples). But when we, as naïve readers, go to these verses, we realize, at least subconsciously, that these proofs involve wrenching distortions from the obvious meaning of the Torah. And that leads us back to our original fear, that death is the end.

A short story from our debate illustrates this anxiety feedback loop:

> The sons of Rabbi Hiyya went out to cultivate their property, and they began to forget their learning. They tried very hard to recall it.
>
> Said one to the other, "Does our [dead] father know our trouble?"
>
> "How should he know," replied the other, "seeing that it is written, 'His sons come to honor and he know it not?'"
>
> Said the other to him: "But does he not know? Is it not written: 'But his flesh grieveth for him, and his soul mourneth over him?' And R. Isaac said [commenting on this]: 'The worm is as painful to the dead as a needle in the flesh of the living?'
>
> [He replied]: "It is explained that they know their own pain, they do not know the pain of others."

In this context, it's forgetfulness that introduces the subject of dying. Unfortunately, we all understand the connection between memory loss and death. As we approach old age and death, we fear senility, and, even more, fear that death will become the ultimate destroyer of memory. In that light, it is understandable that Rabbi Hiyya's sons' first thought, when they start to forget, is about death. They wonder if their dead father "knows" their troubles. They also, most likely, contemplate their own deaths, and start wondering whether, when they die, they'll "know." They first attempt to answer their question the old-fashioned way: with competing Biblical verses. But they hit the anxiety loop. They recall a verse ("His sons come to honor and he know it not") with the clear meaning that the dead are not conscious (and these verses are not hard to find, because, on the surface at least, many verses in the Hebrew Bible reject the idea of an afterlife). And this verse causes anxiety: when we die, we won't *know*. So they find another verse ("But his flesh grieveth for him, and his soul mourneth over him."), but this text leaves us uneasy for two reasons. First of all, because it requires such a bizarre exegesis that we can't help thinking: If the Bible really assures us of an afterlife, why would we need such exaggerated interpretations? Secondly, because even if we go along and accept the weird interpretation, we learn that our afterlives may not only be painful cognitively (we'll "know" our children's troubles), but *physically*. Rabbi Hiyya's sons turn to the Bible for reassurance, but in the end their search creates as much anxiety as their initial question, both for them and for us.

So now our debate leaves the realm of biblical interpretation and switches to an equally valid mode of arguing: anecdote. In other words, the Talmud tells us some ghost stories. The first short narrative doesn't solve much, but it does heal some of our anxieties. I call this one: "The Story of Rabbi Ze'iri and his Landlady."

> Come and hear; for Ze'iri deposited some money with his landlady, and while he was away visiting Rab, she died.
>
> So he went after her to the cemetery and said to her, "Where is my money?"
>
> She replied to him: "Go and take it from under the ground, in the hole of the doorpost, in such and such a place. And tell my mother to send me my comb and my tube of eye-paint by the hand of So-and-so who is coming here tomorrow."
>
> Does not this show that they know?
>
> Perhaps Dumah [an angel of death] announces to them beforehand.

Here, we see communicating with the dead is as routine as dialing a cellphone. You need information, you go to the cemetery, you speak. The story portrays the world of the dead as a conspicuously ordinary place, where you brush your hair in the morning, put on eye make-up, and where it pays to pack an overnight bag. This exchange removes some of the daunting strangeness from death. The spirits there are like us, the passage teaches. They use combs and eyeliner. After reading this, we find ourselves less afraid.

But the most striking thing about the passage is the Talmud's resistance to its obvious conclusion. If Ze'iri can march right up to a tombstone and chat with his dead landlady, then our question is answered. The dead "know"; they hear us when we speak, and even answer our questions. But the Talmud ignores the remarkable fact of communication between worlds, and focuses on the more narrow issue of how the landlady "knows" that "so-and-so" is about to die. Instead of concluding the debate and declaring Rabbi Hiyya the winner, the Talmud suggests that the landlady heard about the death from Dumah, an angel who can freely travel between the worlds. The dead, in other words, don't necessarily "know" directly; they simply learn information from an angel.

I suspect there are good reasons why the Talmud is reluctant to come to the obvious conclusion from this story that the dead do "know." I'll discuss these reasons in a few paragraphs. For now, let me suggest that here at least the Talmud isn't interested in the banal "knowing" about where's the money, or instructions to bring combs and eye make-up. We can assume that the dead know about these things. What the Talmud really wants to discover is if the dead know about more important matters – like, for instance, life and death. The story leaves this issue unresolved. Maybe Ze'iri's landlady knew about the upcoming death because "they know." They leak through. Or maybe they don't. Maybe they don't know anything unless Dumah tells them.

The next story also leaves the overall issue unresolved, but still provides some relief from our anxieties about death.

Come and hear: The father of Samuel had some money belonging to orphans deposited with him. When he died, Samuel was not with him, so they called Samuel, "The son who steals the money of orphans."

So Samuel went after his father to the cemetery, and said to them [the dead], "I am looking for Abba." [Samuel's father's name was Abba.]

They said to him: "There are many Abbas here."

"I want Abba the son of Abba," he said. [Samuel's grandfather was also named Abba.]

They replied: "There are also several Abbas the son of Abba here."

He then said to them: "I Want Abba the son of Abba the father of Samuel; where is he?"

They replied: "He has gone up to the Academy of the Sky."

…Meanwhile his father came. Samuel observed that he was both weeping and laughing. He said to him: "Why are you weeping?"

He replied: "Because you are coming here soon."

"And why are you laughing?"

"Because you are highly esteemed in this world."

…Samuel then said to him: "Where is the money of the orphans?"

He replied: "Go and you will find it in the case of the millstones. The money at the top and the bottom is mine; that in the middle is the orphans'."

He said to him: "Why did you do it like that?"

He replied: "So that if thieves came, they should take mine, and if the earth destroyed any, it should destroy mine."

Does not this show that they know?

Perhaps Samuel was exceptional: as he was esteemed, they proclaimed beforehand, "Make way [for him]!"

Once again, in judging the debate, the Talmud ignores Samuel's remarkable rise to Heaven, and his lengthy conversation with the mysterious folks who guard the gate. Ordinary conversations between the living and the dead don't seem to matter here. Instead, the Talmud focuses on Abba's knowledge that Samuel will soon die. But, again, according to the Talmud, this "knowing" doesn't prove anything. Maybe Abba only knew about the upcoming death because Samuel was a celebrity. You can't learn from an exception, in this case the famous and esteemed Samuel. Maybe they announce all celebrities before they enter the next world.

So the story doesn't give a definitive answer, but it does offer comfort. Primarily, it teaches that relationships survive death. This message comes through with a bit of word play. Samuel goes to the cemetery and asks for "Abba," which was his father's first name, but it's also Hebrew for "father." As far as the gatekeepers were concerned, Samuel might very well have been saying, "I'm looking for father," to which they respond, "There are a lot of fathers (Abbas) here." This teaches us that relationships survive death. Your father may be dead, the story is telling us, but he's still your father. "There are many fathers here." Everyone in the next world who was once a father on Earth is *still* a father.

For me, personally, this means that my late father is still my father, even though he died many years ago. And I'm still his son. I imagine Samuel walking over to the graveyard not just with the intention of speaking to his father, but also wondering if, in any real sense, he still has a father. After all, his father is dead. But he gets an answer, an answer we can all appreciate: "There are many fathers here."

The text is even more comforting because it teaches that not only do our relationships survive, but they also retain an emotional intensity. Samuel's father still cries for his son, and still laughs for him. Emotions transcend the border between this world and the next. They leak through. Heaven, in this story, is filled with souls that laugh and/or cry about the folks back home. Not only do combs and eye make-up survive the transition from life to death (not to mention hair and eyes), but also the deep feelings which define our relationships. This is a soothing message because, even if you dismiss this bizarre tale as nothing but a ghost story, for many of us, the message rings true. I may never receive the privilege of journeying to heaven to ask my father where he hid the money, but I do feel that I still love him, that I'm his son, he's my father, and that he still loves me. I feel all these things to be true, even if I can't possibly prove them. The story of Samuel's father – the story of Abba – validates my instincts and emotions. When I visit either of my parent's graves and start talking (I don't ask them where they hid the money), part of me feels ridiculous, but part of me embraces the act as an authentic form of communication. I'm demonstrating an essential truth. They're dead, but they're still my parents. And I'm still their son. That sentiment comforts me, heals me.

But the most healing tale, albeit the most difficult and frankly ridiculous, is the second in the series, a narrative I call "The Story of the Pious Man, His Fight with His Wife, and the Two Ghosts." It's a lengthy passage, but it pays to quote it in full.

It is related that a certain pious man gave a denar [a valuable coin] to a poor man on the eve of New Year in a year of drought, and his wife scolded him, and he went and passed the night in the cemetery, and he heard two spirits conversing with one another.

Said one to her companion, "My dear, come and let us wander about the world and let us hear from behind the curtain what suffering is coming upon the world."

Said her companion to her, "I am not able, because I am buried in a matting of reeds. But you go, and whatever you hear tell me."

So the other went and wandered about and returned.

Said her companion to her, "My dear, what have you heard from behind the curtain?"

She replied, "I heard that whoever sows after the first rainfall will have his crop smitten by hail."

So the man went and did not sow till after the second rainfall, with the result that everyone else's crop was smitten and his was not smitten.

The next year he again went and passed the night in the cemetery, and heard the two spirits conversing with one another. Said one to her companion, "Come and let us wander about the world and hear from behind the curtain what punishment is coming upon the world."

Said the other to her, "My dear, did I not tell you that I am not able because I am buried in a matting of reeds? But you go, and whatever you hear, come and tell me."

So the other one went and wandered about the world and returned.

She said to her, "My dear, what have you heard from behind the curtain?"

She replied, "I heard that whoever sows after the later rain will have his crop smitten with blight."

So the man went and sowed after the first rain with the result that everyone else's crop was blighted and his was not blighted.

Said his wife to him, "How is it that last year everyone else's crop was smitten and yours was not smitten, and this year everyone else's crop is blighted and yours is not blighted?" So he related to her all his experiences.

The story goes that shortly afterwards a quarrel broke out between the wife of that pious man and the mother of the [deceased] child, and the wife said to the mother, "Come and I will show you your daughter buried in a matting of reeds."

The next year the man again went and spent the night in the cemetery and heard those conversing together.

One said, "My dear, come and let us wander about the world and hear from behind the curtain what suffering is coming upon the world."

Said the other, "My dear, leave me alone; our conversation has already been heard among the living."

This would prove that they know?

Perhaps some other man after he died went and told them.

What an odd little story. But, for me, it speaks powerfully to my own complex emotions about death and dying. On the one hand, it reinforces some of my pet anxieties. One of the ghosts in the story is improperly buried and therefore stuck in a kind of limbo, unable to visit either side of the curtain. She's a Talmudic Deadman (really, a Deadwoman or Deadgirl), who is left stranded in nowhere until her mother can find her the proper burial clothes.

I had actually read this story years before Marcello Rothstien invaded my dreams and accused me of screwing up his burial, but I only recently discovered how well it confirms my nearly obsessive fears about making mistakes at funerals. One slip, and the dead soul can't tour through "the suffering that comes upon this world."

There is also an eerie parallel between Judith Rothstien's fear (which later became my own) of Marcello "leaking through," and one of the ghost's easy access to our side of the curtain. In the story, there's not much to keep the dead away from this world. There's a lot of leaking through.

On the other hand, this is not a scary story. On the contrary, it's one of the least frightening ghost stories I've ever read. Yes, the dead leak through, but when they do, the live hero gets rich. Burial mistakes can trap spirits in a kind of limbo, but these mistakes, apparently, are easily correctible. And death, in the story, is a lark. You make friends, zip around the universe exploring Earth's disasters, without, at least not in this particular story, suffering their consequences. Here, the afterlife is not only reassuringly normal, a place where you might need to touch up your eye make-up, or comb your hair, or laugh about your children, it's also an adventure, where drought and blight are part of a tourist drama, available for your amusement. There's no reason to fear death or the dead after reading this story (or any of these stories, for that matter). The pious man who spends the night in the cemetery after quarreling with his wife is never spooked. He comes back, every year, to hear more insider trading tips from his new dead friends.

Of course, no one can sustain this jolly view of death for long. Shortly after closing the Talmud, some of our old fears will emerge (mine certainly do). That's not surprising. Fear of death is simply innate; the funniest, most healing stories won't ever rob death of its power to scare us. The Talmud, in particular, remains conflicted. Despite all the evidence from these narratives, it can't bring itself to reach the obvious conclusion: the dead "know"; there is a rich and meaningful communication between both sides of the curtain. After several pages, the Talmud simply drops the argument, leaving it unresolved. Probably, the rabbis didn't want to commit themselves to either side because of their own anxieties. They didn't want to decide authoritatively that the dead "know," because they were afraid of the same "leaks" that plagued Judith Rothstien. Ghosts still frighten us, even after we read about the good-natured adventurers in our little story. But the Talmud also resists concluding that the dead *don't* "know," because that would mean the end of all "knowledge," of emotions, of consciousness, of everything.

So, ultimately, the Talmud decides not to decide. In rabbinic jargon, the quarrel remains a *teku*, a dispute without resolution. According to rabbinic lore, Elijah the Prophet will appear at the end of time to resolve all *tekus*. None of us, of course, will have to wait that long to find out.

Obsessions

Recently, some of my congregants accused me of being obsessed with death. I was initially shocked to hear this accusation (who *me?*), but, after listening to several complaints, I had to admit that they might have a point. Over the years, I have offered several adult education classes about death; and taught it as a subject in our Hebrew High. I often lecture on the subject around town. This past year, my principal High Holiday sermon was about the after-life. Apparently, I've alarmed a few listeners. One young woman complained about a sermon I'd given a few weeks before where

I'd told the story of a grieving mother who'd jumped into an open grave, and started pulling down dirt on herself so she could be buried along with her baby daughter. (Charming story, isn't it?) I told the congregation that I had some remote sympathy for the impulse. Death, I said, can often seem like a respite from a harsh world. I admitted that on occasion I'd looked at open graves with something like envy. "Maybe you have, Rabbi," the young woman commented, "but most of us haven't. None of us can ever imagine jumping into an open grave, and then burying ourselves alive. Maybe this is your issue."

Maybe. I rather doubt that it's just my issue, but I do admit to thinking about death quite a bit, wondering what it's really like. My younger son Ilan, as it happens, went through a similar obsession right after my mother died. The major difference was that he was three years old, and got over it pretty quickly, while I'm still stuck, Deadman-like, in my morbid fascination. Still, I found his journey fascinating.

My older son Benjamin was six when my mother died. My mother was close with both boys, but I expected Benjamin to respond more dramatically since he was old enough to understand what was happening. I doubted Ilan would even remember my mother after a year. But Benjamin rarely mentioned his grandmother after she died, while Ilan kept talking about her for two years. He also developed a raging curiosity about death. For the first sixth months after my mother passed away, not a day would go by without Ilan peppering me with questions. Following my own inclinations, at first I answered him as directly as possible. I told him that our bodies die, but the soul, the most important part of ourselves, goes to Heaven and spends time with God. I expected the very specific and concrete nature of my replies would put the matter to rest. He'd asked a question – what happens when we die? – and I'd answered, with no beating around the bush. Instead he followed through with the tenacity of a bulldog. Where is Heaven? (Actually, he used the word "Heavens." For years, he insisted on using the plural when talking about Heaven.) I'd point, and say "up there." But that's the sky, he'd point out. Grandma's in the sky? Uh, no, I'd say. Heaven is, well, above the sky. Above the sky? In outerspace? Even higher, I'd answer. What's higher than heavens? he'd demand. Nothing, I'd say, injecting as much confidence as I could muster into my response, trying to sound completely sure.

But isn't God higher than Heavens?

No, God is *in* Heaven.

He'd give me a break for a few seconds, and then correct me. "God's not in heavens. Grandma's in heavens. God's even *higher* than heavens." Then he'd look straight up at the ceiling, contemplating the Universe, before looking at me again.

"Can Grandma talk there?"

"Yes, she can talk."

"With her mouth?"

"Yes, with her mouth."

"They have mouths in heavens?"

"Yes, they do."

"And teeth."

"Yes, and teeth."

"Eyes?"

"Yes."

"Fingers?"

"Fingers."

"She can talk?"

"Yes, she can talk."

"With her mouth?"

"Yes, she uses her mouth."

"Is there a tongue in her mouth?"

Queries about communication and body parts seemed to go hand in hand (so to speak). His curiosity about talking reminded me of the Talmud's discussion about "knowing." Both the Talmud and my three-year-old son were concerned about the levels of consciousness we retain after we die, indeed about the nature of consciousness itself. For Ilan, the act of speaking was equivalent to the Talmud's "knowing." If we couldn't speak, then we couldn't know, and if that was the case, how can there be existence of any kind – either during or after life – without consciousness? Like the Talmud, Ilan moved easily from the abstract to the concrete. He fussed a lot about talking, but also asked about toes and teeth. I was tempted to tell him that the dead use eye make-up and combs.

He also asked me how long we had to stay in Heaven after we died. I told him forever.

"How long is forever?"

"A really, really long time."

"More than infinity years?" Someone, probably his brother, had introduced him to the word infinity. Not surprisingly, he found it useful in these discussions.

"Exactly. Infinity years," I answered.

"And what happens after infinity years?"

I thought of telling him there's no such thing as "after infinity years," but as long as I was hewing to the traditional and the concrete, I plunged forward into more Jewish teachings. "We come back to life here," I said. "God gives us our bodies, and we come back."

He shut up for a few minutes, playing that shocking bit of news over in his mind. Then he resumed the interrogation with renewed force.

"Will Grandma be sick when she comes back?"

"No, she'll be better."

"What about her brain?" (She died of a brain tumor.)

"Her brain will be well."

"What about her toes?"

"She'll have all her toes."

It wasn't the variety of questions that so exhausted my wife and myself during this strange, awful period. It was his dogged repetitiveness. We would answer a question, and he'd ask it again, a week later, or a day later, an hour later, two minutes later. He could spend twenty minutes alone on questions about body parts at the resurrection, fussing over eyes and toes and teeth. We understood what was going on. He was seeking reassurance. His father's mother had just died, opening the possibility that his father or mother could die, or that he would one day die. Those are frightening thoughts for a three-year-old, or for anyone. But I detected very little fear in Ilan's questions. More plain curiosity. He was like the Talmud. Anxiety fueled some of his inquiry, but mostly he displayed the same spiritual inquisitiveness that drives all metaphysical seekers. Do they know? Will we know? Like the Talmud, he was extremely reluctant to end the debate.

He didn't just pose questions. He developed theories, and held forth on the subject, in ways unique to a three-year-old. For example, he had a doll named Ilana, but after my mother passed away, he renamed her Ilana Died. She'd come back to life, he explained, after dying and then spending infinity years in heavens. He pointed out to me her fingers, toes, eyes, and ears, all of which had survived the transition intact. He made up a game with his brother called "Baby," where each boy took turns role-playing in an elaborate family fantasy. The premise, rather like a situation comedy, was a single father raising a baby. What happened to the mother? She died. Once, I overheard Ilan teling a pre-school friend about the afterlife. How do you know this? his friend demanded. From my father, Ilan explained. "He read about it in the Torah." (I don't recall invoking the authority of the Torah, but who knows?)

Five months after my mother died, and two weeks before my own family was scheduled to fly to Israel for a month-long visit, Ilan began singing a song he made up called "Gonna Die." The first version went, "Mommy's gonna die in fifteen days," which he'd repeat over and over. He sang the song to us everywhere, at home, in restaurants, at the mall, in the back of the car. Later he added the lines, "Daddy's gonna die in fifteen days," and then "Benjamin's gonna die in fifteen days," then "I'm gonna die in fifteen days." Not to put too fine a point on it, this freaked us out. It was one thing to ask about toes and eyes in the afterlife, but quite another to predict death for a family about to fly on an El Al jet to Israel. We began paying extremely close attention to the political situation in Israel. My wife also looked up El Al's flight safety record (which turned out to be excellent). Neither my wife nor I admitted to any real fright, though I, for one, breathed a sigh of relief after fifteen days.

It may not surprise you to learn that I enjoyed talking to Ilan about death, enjoyed answering his questions, listening to his various theories. The last time we had a serious talk on the subject was two years ago. He asked me *how* do people die? I started to give him a medical response, telling him that our hearts stop pumping blood to our brains, but I quickly realized he wasn't asking a biological question. He was interested in a different mechanics; he wanted to know how our souls got to Heaven. He was ten years old, more sophisticated, but still a child. He could handle abstract concepts. He understood as much as anyone can the concept of the invisible soul. He stopped asking about teeth and mouth. He pronounced Heaven correctly. We talked for a few minutes, and he told me he'd like to see Heaven, but isn't anxious to go any time soon. I told him I agreed completely. I enjoyed the discussion. I thought of asking him if he's afraid of death, and if that's why he thinks about it so much. But I didn't want to be the one to introduce fear into our conversations. He didn't need me to remind him that the idea of death can be scary.

I enjoyed those discussions, and I also enjoy studying the Talmud's stories and reflections on death and dying. And I like teaching and speaking about death, and offering workshops on death and dying in the Jewish tradition. I guess my congregants are correct; I am a bit obsessed.

But I don't want you to get the wrong idea. There's a character in the movie "Harold and Maud" who's so obsessed with death, she shows up at the funerals of complete strangers. I'm not that character. In fact, here's a secret: I don't like funerals. Officiating at funerals is one of my least favorite professional activities. And you've already guessed why. I'm afraid of making mistakes. The last thing I want to do is trap some poor soul on the wrong side of the curtain.

Chapter 3

HOMELESS

The Massachusetts Turnpike

Sometime in October, 2001, about a month after my father died, I was driving on the Massachusetts Turnpike when a song came on the radio that forced me to pull over. The song was "Homeless" by folksinger Loudon Wainright III, and it was about mourning his mother, who'd recently passed away. Several lines rang so true, I felt as if I had been punched in the chest. For instance: "Good friends call and ask if I'm fine/ I tell them I am, but I'm not. It's a line." Or: "They say in the end your good friends pull you through/ But everyone knows my best friend was you." But the line that literally forced me off the road, because I could no longer trust myself to drive through tears, was: "You're why I've done this all this time/ But now playing and singing seems like a game or a crime." I later learned, though I guess I figured it out by listening to the song, that Wainright's mother had been a folksinger and songwriter, and that her example motivated his career more than anything else. He watched her sing professionally as a child, and decided that would be his career too. But, as he sang to me through my radio, now she's gone. So, what now?

I became a rabbi because of my father. That's not how I've answered the question the hundreds of times people have asked me: "Why did you become a rabbi?" (or other variations of the question, such as, "Is this a job for a nice Jewish boy?" or "You're doing *what*?" or "What the hell?"). It's certainly not what I wrote on my application to rabbinic school, where I described theological struggles and living in Israel and commitment to Jewish education and love of the Talmud (blah, blah, blah). It's not what I told the many nice people who interviewed me for jobs over the years, where I mainly skirted the question and talked about how badly I'd always wanted to work at…(whichever place I was applying to work at) or work for…. (whoever I was applying to work for). If anything, I occasionally mentioned my grandfather, the "other" Rabbi Philip Graubart, whom I never met, or even, God help me, my great-grandfather, Rabbi Judah Loeb Graubart, former chief rabbi of Toronto, or his father, Rabbi Binyomin Graubart of Staszow, Poland, as if these ghostly presences pushed me along more than my living, breathing father.

I probably sort of believed some of those responses, though not long ago, I dug out my application essays, and was so embarrassed by my answers, I shoved the pages back in the drawer after five minutes.

It is true. I did become a rabbi because of my father. He influenced my choice in such an overwhelming and definitive way that there was really no "choice." Do we *choose* to do the only thing we could possibly do? Is destiny ever a choice? Anyway, it doesn't matter anymore; I became a rabbi because of him, if not for him.

Not only that, I seem to have mimicked many of the patterns of his career. Like him, after about ten years in the pulpit, I looked for non-pulpit jobs. I seriously considered Hillel because he had been a Hillel director. Over the years, I've applied to one job that he once held, and two that he also applied for, including my current job. I have also used many of his ideas – on synagogue management, theology, rabbinic priorities, developing a pastoral persona. I learned about professional distance from him; I mirror his defensive cynicism. People tell me that my speaking style matches his, the way I wave my arms, grip the podium, my rush to spit out the words. I even followed his casket to Southern California; he's buried in Los Angeles, I live in San Diego. I've followed him my entire professional life. But now, like Loudon Wainright's folk-singing mom, he's dead. So, now what?

Jacob and Joseph – The Similarities

Fathers influence sons so frequently and so powerfully in the book of Genesis, that my father (who else?) once taught me that you could call it "The Book of Fathers and Sons." This theme is most evident in the patriarchal narratives. Isaac, for example, makes his fortune re-opening the wells his father Abraham had once dug. Jacob, like his father Isaac, ends his life blind, and blessing his children. He even crosses his hands to bless his grandchildren, favoring the younger over the older, in much the same way that his blind father had favored him, even though he was the younger sibling. There are several other subtle and not-so-subtle examples of Abraham pushing Isaac, and Isaac pushing Jacob.

But the most powerful influence is that of Jacob over his eleventh son Joseph. Some similarities in their lives are obvious. Both fight with siblings, and for both, the squabbling forces them to leave their homes. Both make their fortunes away from the land of Israel, Jacob in Aram, Joseph in Egypt. Both start off as paupers, but then, after years of struggle, both become rich and powerful.

Both are deceivers. Jacob deceives his brother and lies to his father. Joseph pretends not to recognize his brothers, then plays an elaborate hoax on them. Both are victims of deception. Laban, Jacob's father-in-law, tricks him into marrying the wrong sister. Joseph's brothers deceive his father into thinking that his youngest son had been killed by a wild animal.

Dreams play an important role for both Jacob and Joseph; in fact, for both father and son, dreams are directly connected to their ambitions and good fortunes. Jacob dreams that God, standing on top of a ladder, tells him that he will "burst forth, North, South, East, and West"[1] and be a father of a great nation. Later,

1. Genesis 28:14.

Jacob learns from a dream how to acquire the great majority of his father-in-law's livestock. Joseph dreams that his brothers' sheaves bow down to his, and later that, the "sun, the moon, and eleven stars"[2] all bow down to him. Later, because he interprets the dreams of the butler and the baker, Joseph is brought before Pharaoh, and shortly thereafter, he becomes Prime Minister of Egypt because of his interpretation of Pharaoh's dreams.

A less obvious similarity is the way they both transform themselves later in their lives. For both, the early symbols of their raw ambition become instruments for helping others. Jacob begins his adult life obsessed with blessing. He steals his brother's blessing, deceiving his father in the process. Later, through sheer physical strength, he forces God's angel to bless him. For Jacob, blessings represent status, success, power. Isaac's blessing promises him dominion over his brother, as well as "the fat of the Earth, abundance of new grain and wine."[3] The younger Jacob will do anything – steal, lie, and scrape – for that blessing.

But as an older man, Jacob becomes the Bible's foremost bestower of blessings. Actually, it starts right after his wrestling match with the Angel. In the next scene, he encounters his long-estranged brother Esau, the man from whom he'd stolen his father's blessing. After bowing down numerous times to Esau, and embracing him, Jacob says *"kach na 'et birchati,"* or "Take my blessing."[4] Many translators render *"birchati"* as "my gift" – Jacob does offer his brother a substantial gift – but the word literally means "my blessing." It's hard not to read this scene as Jacob symbolically returning the blessing he had stolen all those years ago. By the end of his life, Jacob becomes positively promiscuous in giving out blessings.

When Joseph takes his father to meet Pharaoh, Jacob blesses him twice, once in greeting (Genesis 47:7), and once in farewell

2.   Ibid. 37:9.
3.   Ibid. 27:28.
4.   Ibid. 33:11.

(v. 10). In the next chapter he blesses Joseph, and then immediately blesses Joseph's sons, famously crossing his hands, so the right hand, that is the stronger blessing, falls on the second born Ephraim, while the left hand, the weaker blessing, goes to the first-born Menashe. (Here Jacob once again imitates his father Isaac who gave the younger Jacob the stronger blessing, and the elder Esau the weaker one). The following chapter contains the Bible's longest sustained blessing up to that point – Jacob blessing all his sons. He actually ends his life with words of blessing. Jacob goes from being a taker of blessing – by nook or by crook – to a man who bestows blessings with his very last breath. In other words, he begins life focused on his own ambitions, but ends up facilitating the ambitions of others.

Joseph undergoes a similar change. His early raw ambitions are symbolized by dreams. He dreams that everyone and everything ("the sun, the moon, the stars") will bow down to him. It's not hard to interpret those dreams; his brothers and his father understand immediately what they mean: Joseph is ambitious, he wants to rule. His early dreams represent his own narcissism, his relentless desires. But, upon his arrival in Egypt, Joseph changes. He becomes the Bible's premier interpreter of dreams.

The Talmud has an interesting take on dream interpretation: "The dream follows the interpreter."[5] In other words, dreams end up meaning whatever the interpreter says they mean. Reality follows interpretation, giving the interpreter a great deal of power. In a Talmudic tale, the sages Abaye and Raba each consult a dream interpreter named Bar Hedya, but only Abaye pays him. They both dream that they had to recite the verse: "Your ox shall be slain before your eyes." Bar Hedya tells Abaye that it means his business will prosper, while he tells Raba that his business will fail. Both interpretations come true. Dreams follow the interpreter.

Joseph became an interpreter, and thereby helped others. He interpreted the butler's dream, and Pharaoh released him

---

5. Talmud B. *Berachot* 47A.

from prison (he didn't do so well for the baker). He interpreted Pharaoh's dream and rescued a civilization. He goes from being a ruthless young man obsessed with his own dreams, to an interpreter facilitating great dreams for others.

We can also identify clear turning points for both Joseph and Jacob – two similar incidences that change their focus from intensely inward to outward, where they go from being takers to givers. For Jacob, it's wrestling with the Angel. Though he extorts a blessing and earns the name Israel, he comes away from the battle with a wound, a limp, and a new orientation. By the next scene, this new Jacob, now named Israel, returns the stolen blessing to Esau. Later he concludes the book of Genesis with a long series of blessings.

For Joseph, it's the scandal with the wife of his employer Potiphar. She tries to seduce him, but he resists. Finally, she grabs his cloak, frames him for attempted rape, and has him tossed in the dungeon. There, chastened, he becomes a dream interpreter. He focuses on others' dreams, not his own. Both Jacob and Joseph literally hit rock bottom, Jacob falling to the earth in a cosmic wrestling match, and Joseph landing on the cold dungeon floor. Then both arise as different men.

All these similarities. Genetics? Mimicry? Coincidence? When Isaac uncovers his father's wells, he's consciously striding in his father's footsteps, digging around for nuggets of Abraham's life, seeking both guidance and independence, continuity and distance. But Joseph never seems to be intentionally imitating his father. When his brothers sell him into slavery, he's an altogether self-absorbed young man. It's hard to imagine him with any gift for evaluating the character of others, even his own father. Besides, many of these episodes simply *happen* to Joseph. He's sold into slavery, framed for rape, consulted about dreams. His father seems more of a ghostly presence than an actual influence. In fact, in a Midrash, a vision of Jacob pops up before Joseph's eyes, at the same moment that Potiphar's wife demands that he sleep with her. In this version, Joseph so desires his boss' wife that "he could feel his semen between his fingers."[6] He's about to commit adultery with her when the ghostly image appears, and dissuades him. Joseph doesn't consciously reflect much on his father, or consciously consider what he thinks his father would want him to do. The point of the Midrash is that Jacob's influence on Joseph is extremely subtle, as if it's an insubstantial ghost doing the influencing, not a real person.

Dad and Me – The Similarities

I became a rabbi because of my father. It was my destiny. I say this now, at a distance of over twenty years. But it's not that simple. For me, my father's example was mostly an unconscious pull, tugging an invisible cord. Up until the day before I decided to apply for rabbinical school, my father never once suggested that I become a rabbi. In fact, several times during my high school and college years, he actually went out of his way to dissuade me from becoming a rabbi, sometimes jokingly, often seriously. But, back then, it didn't matter, because I didn't have the slightest intention of becoming a rabbi. I had other plans – big plans. But plans fall through. I applied to rabbinical school after dropping out of graduate school and giving up on living in Israel. I became a rabbi, in other words, because I'd failed at those things that I really wanted to accomplish. I became a rabbi because I needed to do something, and I didn't know what else to do. I told this story in an earlier chapter, but for now, it's important to understand that I didn't in any way set out to follow my father's example.

But follow him I did, and not just to rabbinical school. Like Jacob and Joseph, my father's life mysteriously asserted itself many times, leading me along paths I thought I'd carved myself, but that he'd actually beaten out before me. For example:

1. After ten years in the pulpit, I decided I'd had enough. I considered several Hillel positions on college campuses,

6. Talmud B. *Sotah* 36B.

but ended up taking a job as an educator and programmer at the National Yiddish Book Center. My father also gave up on pulpit life after exactly ten years. He became a Hillel Director.

2. Despite my resolution never to return to the pulpit, after one year at the Yiddish Book Center, I became a pulpit rabbi again, in San Diego, California. It took my father a little longer, but he also returned to the pulpit after vowing to stay away. His first return also took him to Southern California. He actually died still a pulpit rabbi, in Chicago.

3. Both of us went through significant political shifts. It's hard for me to write this as an influence since I can't imagine my own political thinking as anything but authentically my own. Still, the similarity is interesting. As a young graduate student, and then rabbinical student, I identified myself as a neo-Conservative. I voted for Ronald Reagan (this might be the most embarrassing personal revelation in this book). I anxiously awaited every issue of *Commentary* Magazine. I'm now a left of center Democrat, and could not imagine myself voting for any Republican. I read *Tikkun* Magazine. My father supported Richard Nixon. He loved quoting Barry Goldwater and William Buckley. He introduced me to *Commentary* Magazine and *The National Review*. But he died a liberal. He spent the last 10–15 years of his life working with Gay activists and advocates for the homeless. He shocked me in one of our last conversations by complaining about Israel's "bullying." In his politics, he was more flamboyant, radical, dramatic, and confrontational than I, but that was true of everything. We still trod a parallel path, which, I suppose is just a poetic way of saying I did what he did, and thought what he thought.

4. We both started out disdaining the Jewish Renewal Movement. By the end of his life, though, he'd become the rabbi at a Jewish Renewal-style synagogue. I haven't gone that far (I never go that far), but I've incorporated many Jewish Renewal elements into my own rabbinate, probably more than the great majority

of Conservative rabbis. By the way, both my father and I had pretty much had it with the Conservative movement by the time he died (he more than I).

5. This one's a bit of a stretch. We both lost our parents at fairly young ages. Now, he was nine when his mother died of a burst appendix and fifteen when he lost his father to pneumonia – and I was thirty-seven when my mother died, forty when he died. So he did become an orphan at a much younger age, and his orphanhood significantly influenced his later life and character, unlike my adult orphanhood, which left me sad and bereft, but not fundamentally a different person. Still, my children were young enough when he died that they won't really remember him. He'll be the grandfather they never knew, just like I never knew my paternal grandfather or grandmother.

6. Dare I say this? He was a fine rabbi: personable, interesting, competent, and hard-working. And I? I suppose I am also.

Again, none of this was imitation, and certainly not hero-worship. By the end of his life, I was disappointed in him. Disillusioned. Lacking in respect. He wasn't my leader and I wasn't his follower. I just did so many things that he did.

Jacob and Joseph – The Differences

Of course there were differences. Between myself and my father, and between Jacob and Joseph. Let's start with the two patriarchs:

1. Jacob had thirteen children with four wives; Joseph, just two, with one wife.

2. Jacob became rich and powerful, but not nearly as rich and powerful as Joseph. In fact almost everything about Joseph was more dramatic, more flamboyant.

3. Jacob began his adult life without a penny, but Joseph had it much worse. He was a slave and then a prisoner, tossed into

the dungeon on charges of attempting to rape his master's wife.

4. Jacob, egged on by his mother, tentatively deceived his father, but Joseph seemed to revel in deceiving his brothers, ramping up the stakes with each deception, driving them to utter despair. It's hard to imagine Jacob devising such a baroque series of deceptions. Furthermore, Jacob told a few lies at significant points in his life, but Joseph lived a lie in Egypt, changing his name, raising his sons as Egyptians, telling no one of his origins.

5. Jacob struggled to make it, dogged by a jealous brother and a devious father-in-law. But Joseph, torn from his family, betrayed by his brothers, framed for a crime he didn't commit, didn't just struggle, he *suffered*. The fundamental difference between suffering and struggling – a significant difference – is the difference between the early adult years of Jacob and Joseph.

6. Looking back from a distance, Jacob and Joseph reflected on their early years in markedly different ways. As an old man, this is how Jacob summarized his life to Pharoah: "The years of my sojourn are one hundred and thirty. Few and evil have been the days of my life."[7] Few and evil. All around, that's an astonishing statement. Jacob became wealthy, "bursting" with material goods. He's the first patriarch to give real life to God's promise that his family would become a great nation. Even with his many struggles and disappointments, it's shocking to see him summarize his life as "evil." And, as many commentators have asked, how, at this point in his life, can he complain that his years have been few? How does he know how long he's going to live? In fact, he lived another seventeen years.

Joseph's retrospective view couldn't be more different. When he revealed himself to his brothers, he said, "Do not be distressed

7.   Genesis 47:9.

that you sold me here, for God sent me ahead of you in order to give life…God sent me before you so you could survive on the land, and to keep you alive in a great survival. Now, it wasn't you who sent me here. No, it was God who placed me as a father to Pharaoh, and the lord of his house, and the ruler of all the land of Egypt."[8] Many years later, after Jacob died, he again confided in his brothers: "Don't be afraid. Am I a substitute for God? You thought to do evil to me, but God thought it for good, so I could do what I've done until today – give life to a multitude. So don't be afraid."[9] Joseph's view is as shocking in its generosity as Jacob's is in its bitterness. Joseph, despite his suffering, doesn't see evil in his life; he sees the hand of a loving God. Another way of putting it: Jacob dies a bitter old man. Joseph dies happy.

Dad and I – The Differences

1. My father switched jobs eight times by the time I was twelve. We lived in six different cities. I've held three jobs in my twenty-year career, and only moved once.
2. He was an outgoing person, gregarious to a fault. For a rabbi, I'm fairly shy. In fact, my shyness often comes up in my performance reviews. I doubt it was ever an issue for him.
3. He had six children, with two wives. I have two children, just one wife.
4. Both his parents died when he was still a boy. Mine died when I was well into adulthood. I rarely heard him speak about either of his parents. I can't seem to stop talking about mine.
5. Here's the big one, the one I've been avoiding. I've been faithful to my wife. My father cheated on my mother at least three times, the last one with a woman he eventually married. I found out about the first affair when I was ten years old.

8. Ibid. 45:5, 7–8.
9. Ibid. 50:19–21.

That revelation certainly colored the way I saw him for the rest of his life. In any case, marital fidelity was a pretty big difference between us.

6. I don't know this for a fact, but my guess is that if someone had asked him that last year in Chicago to summarize his life honestly, he probably would have said something very much like Jacob's "evil and short." He was bitter at the end. He avoided socializing, even going out to restaurants. As far as I could tell, he had no friends. Earlier in his life, he loved country music, good novels, politics, restaurants, the Chicago Cubs, tennis, basketball, jogging, a few friends, women. But during his last years, I couldn't point to one thing he really enjoyed, other than ice cream. He lived in the same town as many of his relatives, but he rarely saw them. He never visited his step-mother, who was living near him in a nursing home. He was involved in a lawsuit with his sister, his only sibling. I don't want to take this too far. He didn't lash out at me, and he was kind and loving to all his children, the ones who lived with him and the ones who didn't. He loved and cherished his second wife. His conversation still sparkled. I never stopped asking his advice, which continued to seem sensible, even sage. I liked him until the end (and, of course, I loved him). But his life, frankly, depressed me. It had narrowed to a single point – his drab house in Evanston, and become as cold and gray as a Chicago winter.

Don't get me wrong, I'm not a ray of sunshine myself. I'm no Joseph, seeing the hand of God in all my disappointments. But I've learned to count my blessings. And I try to enjoy myself.

In fact, my father has become a negative example, a cautionary tale, a model of what not to become. I'm not worried about suddenly committing adultery after nearly twenty years of marriage. But that grayness of soul I saw in the last several years of his life, that narrowness of purpose, those are not exactly foreign to me. On some level, this is a vocational risk. Many pulpit rabbis have a hard time pinpointing where their professional obligations end and their socializing begins. All the weddings, bar/bat mitzvahs, charity dinners – am I working or spending time with friends? Or, more likely, have I given up on friendships altogether and limited my social time to parties I'm obligated to attend? Which, at the end of the day, leaves me with a distaste for parties and a yearning for a quiet room and a book. I'm not an outgoing person. I fake it. So I can see myself one day mistaking human companionship for work and drudgery, lumping true friendship together with awkward social performances, and withdrawing altogether. It happened, I believe, to my father, to his great detriment.

My challenge, then, is obvious. In other words, my lesson from the Jacob/Joseph, father/son story is obvious (many biblical lessons are blindingly obvious when you apply them to other people's lives, much less so when you start looking at your own life). I need to transcend my father's example and move from imitation, conscious or otherwise, to independence, or even rejection. I need to go beyond embracing his legacy to creating a legacy of my own.

Joseph imitated his father, whether consciously or unconsciously, but then improved on him. He rejected his father's bitterness, and embraced a startling generosity. I need to appreciate the many ways I've followed my father, the many gifts he has given me. But I also need to study his life and understand what traps to avoid. If I don't reject at least something of his life, I'll end up back at the Massachusetts Turnpike, on the shoulder of the highway, listening to the radio, tears running down my cheeks, paralyzed. I'll never pull back on the road.

An example. Just recently, I ran into someone who asked me if Alex Graubart was my father. I knew what was coming because I've heard it dozens of times. My father had officiated at her bat mitzvah. The woman was now in her late forties, but the lessons he taught her, about Judaism, Torah, life in general, remain the central influences in her life. She sobbed quietly when I told her that he had died. She only knew him for a year, she told me, but no one, other than her parents, had inspired her more.

Now, this was a bit extreme, but I'd heard it before. Because of the many places my father lived, I've run into people from all over the United States who buttonhole me and testify about my father's influence. But this particular incident surprised me a little since I knew what was going on in my father's life the year of her bat mitzvah. His marriage was falling apart. He'd admitted to his board that he'd had an affair with a congregant. His personal and professional lives were about to explode. But somehow he retained his focus, and crafted life-long teachings for a bat mitzvah girl. And, as I said, I've heard dozens of similar testimonials. That's a legacy.

On the other hand, my father caused my mother real pain. He drove her, I think, to consider suicide. I actually found her suicide note when I was ten years old. Panicked, I showed the note to my father who laughed oddly and quickly ran to find my mother, who was, of course, unharmed. Probably she never intended to kill herself, but who writes a suicide note? Someone contemplating suicide very seriously. My father betrayed her and damaged our family. There were mitigating circumstances, which I won't go into right now. But this is obviously a counter-legacy, a cautionary tale, a path to avoid.

Homeless

The name of the Loudon Wainright III song that drove me off the road – the song about losing a parent – is "Homeless." The name suggests becoming unmoored when a parent dies, losing an anchor, being set adrift. "Now I feel like I'm homeless," he sang to his mother, and I broke down crying, on the side of the road. Not long ago, a friend of mine lost his mother. He pointed out to me some lines of a traditional Jewish prayer one says upon visiting the grave of a mother: "It pains me now," we say, addressing ourselves to our late mothers, "to see my road…my path. My travels in this world are unsteady." In other words, "now that you're gone,

I'm wandering. I'm homeless." I appreciate the image, because it's exactly how I felt when my father died. When he was alive, his example – his very being – rooted me to a path, a tradition, a way in the world. With his death, that road, to say the least, became unsteady. I felt like a high-flying kite whose owner just let go. I flew away, then veered right and left, swooping up and down, with no pattern, no control. My travels in the world were unsteady. For a while, anyway.

Or, another way of putting it – paradoxically: I was stuck. It was an inner wandering. I went to work every day, came home every night, but my mind raced out of control. Why am I doing this? Who am I? I definitely need to try something else, but what should I be? A writer? A professor? A race-car driver? A social worker? A film animator? A stand-up comedian? A Christian? Too many choices, of course, meant no choices at all, no external movement, just inner turmoil. Homeless, but stuck. Eventually, I did change jobs, and then again, winding up in Southern California – coincidentally? – about a hundred miles from his final resting place, in a job he'd turned down thirty years before. But I still wandered inside, grasping at rabbinic roles, personae, searching for a firm pastoral identity. I was much less confident now that he was gone. I still felt homeless, stuck.

Even now, as I write these words, I wonder why that was so. True, he was no longer there to give me advice, but I certainly remembered him. Like Jacob to Joseph, his ghostly presence was available to me. I had his example. Several times, I even spoke to him, asking him what to do in particularly thorny situations. His answers, though imaginary, came through with the clarity of a local phone call. So what was the problem? Why did I feel like, in his dying, he let go of my strings?

The problem, I now see, was the negative example, his dark side – the affairs, the narrow focus, the wandering. To be blunt, I didn't want to end up *like* him. I just wanted to *be* him. When he was alive, his powerful living presence resolved the contradiction between role-model and cautionary tale. But his ghost wasn't strong enough to keep the balance. I didn't know whether to turn toward the light or away from the dark. My travels in the world were unsteady. It really wasn't until I stumbled upon the father-son dynamic in the Jacob and Joseph saga that I began to steady myself. I learned what I had to do. Joseph imitated his father, but then improved on him. His astonishing generosity in forgiving his brothers, and interpreting his harsh life as a blessing, didn't come until his father died, until he heard his old father complaining to Pharaoh about his "few and evil years." Jacob's death set Joseph free, to build on his father's legacy with his own creativity, to grab hold of his own strings. Eventually, I also pulled back on the road, turned off the radio, and grasped at my own strings. I found my way home as a rabbi – different from my father, and the same.

PART TWO

Torah in My Life

Chapter 1

GENESIS

B'reishit – Imperfect Repentance

This week's reading contains two ambiguous stories with distinctly unsatisfying endings, particularly with regard to sin and punishment. In the first story, God warns Adam that if he eats from the fruit, he will die "on that day [!]"[1] Yet, Adam doesn't die that day, and God never mentions death as being part of his punishment. In the second story, God tells Cain that his punishment for murdering his brother will be to live a life of "restless wandering" ("*Na v'nod*").[2] Now, first of all, "a life of restless wandering" strikes me as a relatively light punishment for murder. But, more importantly, Cain never seems to wander at all. Three verses later, the Torah tells us that Cain "settles" down[3]; he even marries, has children, and builds a city.

There are several potential explanations for these problems, but one possibility is that both Adam and Cain mitigated their punishments by repenting. And, in fact, the Torah text itself supports this possibility, at least for Cain, when he exclaims "My sin

1. Genesis 2:17.
2. Ibid. 4:12.
3. Ibid. 4:16.

is too great to bear,"[4] meaning that he accepts responsibility and embraces true contrition.

In a provocative Midrash, Cain explains to a curious and somewhat jealous Adam that, after a trial, God forgave him for his crime. In the Midrash, Cain uses two words to describe his encounter with God. He says "*yatzati*," meaning, "I emerged" – I came out of the trauma still intact. And he says "*nitpasharti*," which means, literally, "I became compromised" – I emerged into a *compromised* life; I came out burdened, traumatized, but able to keep going, to lead a somewhat normal life.

But what about Adam? Earlier, the same Midrash (probably written by the same author), describes a similar process where, after a trial, Adam "*yatza b'dimus*," – "he emerged with atonement." This Midrashic comment is particularly interesting because it is the only one to suggest that Adam was forgiven for his sin. Every other aggadic treatment claims that Adam and Eve were severely punished. So this is a fascinating comment. But what exactly does "emerge with atonement" ("*yatza b'dimus*") mean? Obviously it's a lesser form of pardon that even Cain received, since Adam does have to leave Eden. But it implies some kind of atonement.

According to Rashi, Adam received a minimal level of forgiveness for the simple act of standing before God, of accepting some responsibility. Adam's acceptance of responsibility saved his life, but, equally important, it allowed him to "*yatza*" – to emerge from the experience, like Cain, burdened, traumatized, but still able to move on with his life.

This is an exceptionally important lesson in the wake of the High Holidays. Yom Kippur and Rosh Hashanah offer us an idealized vision of atonement, cleansing, and renewal. And this is an important goal. But real life often prevents us from reaching this ideal. Sometimes, in the unruly space between sin and true cleansing, all we can hope for is "*yatza*" – to emerge, and "*p'sharah*" –

4. Ibid. 4:13.

with compromise; that is to emerge from our conflicts and sins burdened, sad, hurt, but still able to live meaningful lives.

Noah – Embracing Limits

Noah's parents greet his birth with great expectations. Explaining his name, his mother says, "this one will comfort (*Yenachamenu*) us from our grief."[5] What is this grief (Hebrew: "*etzev*")? Clearly, Noah's mother is referring to the "*etzev*" God created by imposing a permanent alienation between human beings and nature. As punishment for eating the forbidden fruit, God tells Adam, "You will till the soil with '*etzev*.'"[6]

I've translated "*etzev*" here as grief, but it could easily mean fatigue or malaise. In Eden, Adam and Eve farmed easily, the Earth cooperating fully with their need to feed themselves. But in Noah's time, farming is hard work.

According to Rashi, who quotes the Midrash, Noah responds to the challenges of his time, and invents the plow. In other words, he diagnoses a societal malaise, and prescribes a technological solution. A new machine, a labor-saving device, will relieve society's crippling fatigue.

Now, the plow is a wonderful thing, but here it solves nothing because the problem isn't physical; it's spiritual. The "*etzev*" remains, and God eventually decides to destroy the world.

Noah makes a mistake common to our time. Our own work leads to fatigue, and our capitalistic, hyper-industrious, population often suffers from a work-related malaise. We experience frustration when there is not enough time in the day to achieve our goals. We've become fatigued. In response, our technological geniuses invent labor-saving devices, such as cellphones, handheld computers, and email, which increase our efficiency and, in theory at least, relieve our fatigue. But not only do these new technologies fail to comfort us, they actually increase our anxiety.

5. Genesis 5:29.
6. Ibid. 2:17.

I recently spent a day at the zoo with a friend and her children. She felt confident taking the day off since she'd recently acquired a blackberry, so she could check her email and phone her office. Naturally, she spent the entire day writing emails and making phone calls. Hardly a day off.

Our cultural malaise calls for spiritual, not technological, solutions. When Noah and his family step off the ark, God gives them a blessing similar to the one God gave Adam and Eve – be fruitful, multiply, and conquer the Earth. But now God introduces several limits, such as commanding the survivors not to murder or eat blood.

Understanding limits is the key spiritual ingredient in fighting our "*etzev*." God blesses us with both abilities and ambition, but if we don't embrace limits, we destroy ourselves. The solution is not more plows. The solution is understanding the need to put down the plows.

Lech Lecha – Beyond Freedom

There's an odd phenomenon in the Bible where many stories are told twice, or even three times. For example, Genesis contains two separate creation stories, two flood stories, and two stories of Abraham pretending that Sarah, his wife, is really his sister (and one of Isaac engaging in the same deception). Some scholars explain this "doubling" by invoking the possibility of different biblical authors. I prefer to examine the similarities and differences in each separate telling, and so discover the deeper meaning behind the one story.

This week's reading contains the first of two tellings of the expulsion of Hagar, Sarah's slave and Abraham's concubine. In both versions, Hagar, an Egyptian (in the Midrash, she's Pharoah's daughter), leaves the cruel bondage of Sarah's slavery and encounters an angel in the desert, near a well. There are several differences between the two versions, but the most significant difference lies in the message the angel gives Hagar. In the second version, the angel tells her to continue on to freedom. But in the first, the angel says that God wants her to return to slavery and "suffer under her (Sarah's) hand."[7]

Why tell this story twice? The Bible seems to be saying that, despite the centrality of the Exodus, we shouldn't value freedom at all costs. Sometimes more freedom is appropriate for our lives, but sometimes, depending on the circumstances, we should embrace less freedom. For example most of the founders of modern Israel could have chosen relatively freer and more prosperous lives in America. But they felt that the times, and their particular circumstances, called for less freedom, not more.

Hagar faced a crisis. The two versions of her story suggest that there are two possible responses to every personal crisis. Sometimes, when we feel fed up with our jobs, or our relationships, or our difficult but important spiritual missions, the appropriate response is to run away, and keep running until we feel freer. Freedom, after all, is a good thing. But sometimes, perhaps more often, the appropriate response is to return, despite the limitations in personal freedom, and complete our task.

Vayera – The Pain of Separation

One of the most dominant themes in the book of Genesis is the traumatic separation of children from parents. In this week's reading, Abraham forcibly expels Ishmael, his son. Later, Abraham attempts to sacrifice Isaac, his second son. And although God stops him at the last instant, Abraham and Isaac never speak to each other again, so the experience is still a traumatic separation. In later readings, Rebecca sends her son Jacob away because she's convinced her other son, Esau, is about to kill him. And Joseph's brothers wrench him away from his father Jacob by selling him into slavery.

On the one hand, the Torah seems to be teaching us that separating from parents should be traumatic. If I want to firmly establish my own destiny, I must, at some point, escape the smothering

7.   Genesis 16:9.

influence of my parents. Breaking away, however, takes effort, and it can be painful, even traumatic, but it is sometimes necessary.

On the other hand, the Torah offers two counter-examples, where the parent-child separation is less painful, and even uplifting. When Rebecca's family sends her away to marry Isaac, they offer her a blessing, "May you become a thousand multitudes."[8] And there's a second version of Jacob's leaving, where he's not fleeing, and Isaac blesses him with the words: "May God Almighty bless you and make you fruitful and multiply…and may He give you the blessing of Abraham."[9] In both these instances, blessings, not pain, accompany the separation.

How can parents ensure that when their children leave them, it happens with blessing and not trauma? Both Rebecca and Jacob's blessings invoke the mission God gave Adam and Eve – to be "fruitful and multiply."[10] Furthermore, Isaac, in parting with his son Jacob, specifically mentions the "blessing of Abraham," emphasizing this family's unique mission to spread monotheism across the globe. In other words, upon leaving, Rebecca and Jacob are reminded that they are part of a great and noble enterprise: the building up of the Jewish people.

Similarly, we can instill blessings in our separations by constantly reminding our children that we all, together, continue to fulfill a great destiny: spreading the ideas of Torah. Certainly, our children will carry out that mission in their own unique ways, charting new courses and redefining the Torah's message. One way or another, they will break away from us. But by clearly defining our families' ideals and missions, we can avoid the harsher traumas.

Chaye Sarah – Testing God

In this week's reading, Eliezer, Abraham's servant, finds a bride for Isaac by asking God to send a woman who will not only give

---

8. Genesis 24:60.
9. Ibid. 28:3–4.
10. Ibid. 1:28.

Eliezer a drink, but will also offer to water his animals. If God sends along such a woman, Eliezer promises, he will take her home to Isaac. And, as we all know, Rebecca shows up almost immediately, fulfills Eliezer's conditions, and ends up marrying Isaac. It's a lovely, romantic story, but, oddly, the Talmudic rabbis disapprove of Eliezer's behavior, comparing him to Saul and Yiftach, irresponsible leaders who made irresponsible bargains with God.

Why does the Talmud disapprove? Probably because the Jewish tradition generally condemns testing our personal relationships with God. If Rebecca had not shown up, Eliezer might very well have concluded that God doesn't care, and he would have lost his faith entirely. More seriously, Eliezer is testing his own relationship with God by playing with the lives of others. After all, as the Talmud points out, even a woman who fulfilled Eliezer's conditions might have been entirely inappropriate for Isaac. Eliezer might have confirmed his own private relationship with God, but in the process, could have ruined the lives of Isaac and Rebecca.

My guess is the rabbis were concerned that this type of matchmaking may have led to a halachically improper marriage. For instance, what if a married woman would have showed up, or a half-sister, or a slave, or a *mamzeret* (child of an improper union, such as adultery or incest) – women whom the Torah forbids men from marrying? In that case, Eliezer could only have fulfilled his personal relationship with God by violating communal norms.

In fact, this was precisely the rabbis' problem with Yiftach's behavior. Yiftach promised that if God granted him military victory, he would sacrifice the first thing that walked out of his house. The Talmud objects, "It could have been an unclean thing"[11] and led to Jewishly improper sacrifices. Once again, Yiftach would have affirmed his own spirituality by violating the communal spirituality. And unlike Eliezer's story, this one doesn't end happily.

---

11. Talmud B. *Ta'anit* 15A.

Yiftach's daughter winds up being the first "thing" that leaves his house.

For the Talmud, and therefore for the Jewish tradition, a relationship with God requires a finely tuned balance between the personal and the communal – a dance, where we constantly leap back and forth between personal fulfillment and communal norms (i.e., the Halachah). Ultimately it's wrong – and certainly in violation of the Jewish spirit – to divorce communal needs from our own private spirituality. Eliezer got away with it. Yiftach wasn't so fortunate.

Toldot – The Fight for Authenticity

This week's reading introduces us to the character Jacob. The most dominant theme in Jacob's life is the struggle for blessing. First, he steals his brother's blessing through an astonishing deception, and then he forcefully wrenches a blessing from an angel.

Why is Jacob so obsessed with blessings? Blessings, in the bible, do not convey material advantages. Nor do they, in many cases, accurately predict the future. For instance, the blessing Jacob steals from his brother never comes true.

Obviously, Jacob suffers from an authenticity crisis – an anxious lack of self-confidence, which forces him to seize any advantage that comes his way. If we closely read the story of how Jacob steals his brother's blessing, we see that Rebecca, Jacob's mother, at first suggests that Jacob present himself to Isaac and solicit a blessing without deception. But Jacob has apparently convinced himself that he could never earn the blessing on his own, so he resorts to trickery.

Ironically, stealing the blessing only adds to Jacob's feelings of inauthenticity. How can he internalize words of blessing if he hasn't authentically earned them? That's why, later, he tries to force an angel to bless him, and even later offers to return the blessing to Esau. Jacob is never satisfied with his own achievements.

For better or worse (I'd say mostly for better), the Jews are the people of Jacob. That is, these feelings of inadequacy, followed by anxious striving, are part of our legacy. As a small people, inheritors of the second born Jacob and Isaac, we are never fully convinced of our own authenticity. As a result, we try harder to build holy lives. No Jew should ever claim to another that he or she practices a more authentic Judaism. Rather, we should all, as Jews, strive for a fuller Jewish authenticity.

On a personal level, when I followed my father's footsteps into the rabbinate, I never felt fully adequate, since he was too daunting a model. I, therefore, struggled hard to build my own sense of authenticity. When he passed away, I again faced the challenge of creating my own rabbinic calling, separate from his influence. Since becoming a rabbi, I've never stopped struggling for authenticity. But I find the struggle to be a blessing, not a curse. In any case, it's my legacy, as one of the people of Jacob.

Vayetse – Tough Choices

Our patriarch Jacob spends more time on the road than any other Biblical hero. All of his significant spiritual experiences take place on a journey, either away from home, or back toward home. For instance, in this week's reading, Jacob leaves home, and immediately – on the road, at Beth El – dreams his famous dream of angels ascending and descending. In the course of the dream, God promises Jacob to "protect" him and "return him" home.[12] Astonishingly, when Jacob wakes up, he pledges that he will accept God *if* God "protects" him on the road (*baderech*) and "returns" him home.

Is Jacob really so faithless and arrogant that he would doubt God's explicit promises, and then condition his own obedience on God's actions? Maybe so, but the rabbis of the Midrash read his pledge differently. They say that God promised physical protection, but Jacob asked for moral protection – protection from sin. The Midrash focuses on the word "*baderech*" (on the road). According to the rabbis, Jacob recognizes the moral perils of "the road" –

12. Genesis 28:15.

the illicit temptations, but also the complicated ethical dilemmas. He asks God for help both in avoiding sin, and in navigating the tricky moral issues he knows he'll face outside the protection of his parents' house.

This Midrash works well for Jacob, because he faced more ethically ambiguous issues than possibly any other biblical character; dilemmas that required balancing competing moral values. For example, when stealing the blessing from his brother, he balanced the value of honesty against the preservation of the Jewish people, ultimately rejecting honesty. One might argue that he chose wrongly, but no one can deny that it was a complicated choice, with no right or wrong resolution. Similarly, when he snuck away from Laban, he balanced honesty (again) against preserving his family. Here I would argue that he chose correctly, but it was still, undoubtedly, a difficult decision. Later, in trying to protect his daughter Dina, or raise his son Joseph, Jacob continues to struggle, balancing conflicting ideals, hoping to do the right thing.

The entire Talmud really bases itself on Jacob's life. The Talmud spends very little time on obvious moral teachings; it assumes we already know that it's wrong to steal or lie. Instead, the Talmud helps us think through those difficult times when, for all sorts of reasons, we may have to choose dishonesty, or even choose to kill. Jacob was right to ask for God's guidance in making tough ethical decisions. It's always hard to decide between competing values, and we need all the help we can get.

Vayishlach – The Human Paradox

This week's reading includes the famous wrestling match between Jacob and an angel. Jacob enters this scene with two clear needs: 1.) He is *"levado,"* alone. This is not mere loneliness, but, a powerful, existential loneliness – the same need Adam experienced before God created Eve. 2.) He's desperate for a blessing. He understands that he acquired his previous blessing through deceit, so now he's anxious to earn one on his own merit.

By the end of the story, he has fulfilled these two needs. The angel blesses him by giving him the new name "Israel." And, since God's name (El), is part of this new name, he is now permanently attached to God, and therefore loses his existential loneliness. He's no longer "*levado*," and no longer bereft of blessing. Happy ending? We might make that claim, except for one detail. He limps away from the wrestling match. In other words, he emerges with a wound – an imperfection, or need, which replaces the old wounds, the old imperfections.

In fact, we learn here a paradox of human reality. None of us really feels fulfilled without a mission. But a true mission implies something missing from our lives, a hole we need to fill. So our desires – our needs, our "wounds" – complete us. They give us meaning, a mission. Our imperfections perfect us. The Kabbalah teaches about a primordial explosion – a "shattering of the vessels" which rained imperfection and evil on the Universe. But the shattering created the concept of *Tikkun* – mending, or healing. *Tikkun* gives our lives meaning, by assigning us a sacred task – repairing the world. Without *Tikkun*, we're bereft of meaning. A perfect world would make us incomplete. But the world's imperfections perfect us. Jacob's new name Israel – "Wrestling with God" – teaches that we can only feel fulfilled by continuing to wrestle with life's difficulties. We're not fully human – we don't reach our full human potential – without our wounds.

That's why I've always found that the happiest people are those who are involved in trying to perfect the world. They understand that we don't attain fulfillment merely by solving problems. We find our truest joy in constantly searching for new problems, and consequently new solutions.

Vayeshev – Dreams and Their Interpretation

In this week's reading, Joseph shares his dreams with his brothers: one where their sheaves bow down to his, and the other where the sun, the moon, and eleven stars bow down to him. The brothers already despise Joseph, but these dreams tip their annoyance into rage. Soon, they sell their brother into slavery.

I have two questions. One, why does Joseph share his dreams? He must know that these dreams would only deepen his brothers' aversion. Two, what was it about these dreams in particular that threw the brothers into a murderous rage? How do they move the brothers from an understandable envy to raw hatred?

The Talmud teaches that dreams "follow the interpreter." In other words, for the Talmud, dreams present a kind of raw material that the interpreter molds into reality. It's not the dream itself that determines the future, it's the interpretation.

Therefore, according to some commentators, Joseph presented his dreams to his brothers for them to interpret – giving them the opportunity to mold his dreams into their aspirations. Though it seems far-fetched, the brothers could have responded, "Obviously these dreams mean that we should listen to you more often. We see now that we should pay more attention to your advice. From now on, let's be partners."

Instead the brothers heard Joseph's dreams (possibly because of his tone or inflection) as representing raw, dynamic ambition, unmediated by interpretation. As a result, they now feared him, and this fear fueled their murderous anger.

All this points to a dramatic change Joseph experiences much later in his life. He goes from being an adolescent dreamer to – as a prisoner in Pharoah's dungeon – an interpreter of dreams. In other words, he enters adulthood nurturing his own ego-driven, raw ambitions, but then transforms himself into someone who facilitates the aspirations of others. In the end, in fact, by interpreting Pharaoh's dream, he facilitates the ambitions of the entire Near East, by feeding its population.

Joseph's transformation echoes a similar path traveled by his father Jacob, who begins his adult life striving and scratching for blessings. In other words, he focuses his attention on his own grand ambitions. But he concludes his life as one of the great bestowers of blessing; at the end of Genesis, he offers pages of blessings to his sons.

Chanukah, of course, is a time to move from dark to light. Joseph and Jacob teach us that we reach enlightenment by transcending our own ego-driven ambitions, and helping fulfill the hopes of others, or the greater dreams of our society. The path of raw ambition is often dark. We stumble about, anxious about our future, unsure of why we are not satisfied, and never confident of our fundamental values. But helping others brings us into the light, by clarifying our values and removing our fears. We leave behind the darkness of ego, and step into the light of love.

Miketz – The Path to Healing

In this week's reading, Joseph gives striking names to his sons. He calls his oldest son, Menashe (in English, "forgetfulness"), because "God has allowed me to forget all the trauma from my father's house";[13] and his second son Ephraim ("fruitfulness"), because "God has made me fruitful in the land of my oppression."[14]

These names describe a process of recovery from trauma: forgetting and prospering. We can only recover from all sorts of trauma, from pregnancy, to torture, to battlefield stress, by first erasing the memory – at least partially – and then moving on with our fruitful lives. At first, both Joseph and his brothers successfully erase the memory of their traumatic encounter. Joseph changes his name and becomes an Egyptian; the brothers, back in Canaan, never directly speak of the incident, and never refer to Joseph by name. This "forgetting" allows them to lead meaningful lives as husbands, fathers, and providers.

The problem, of course, is that all traumatic memories eventually reassert themselves. Joseph's memories, in the form of his brothers, literally show up on his doorstep. For us, repressed

13. Genesis 41:51.
14. Ibid. 41:52.

memories leak through, creating different forms of neurosis. Indeed, Joseph seems to go a little crazy after seeing his brothers. He cries uncontrollably – several times – and sends them off on cruel wild goose chases.

Joseph's solution is to develop a third stage in healing after the second stage of prospering: interpretation. Interpretation is Joseph's special gift; it gets him out of prison and makes him prime minister of Egypt. At the end of the story, Joseph fully absorbs his past, but re-interprets the memories. "Don't grieve that you sold me here," Joseph tells his brothers, "for God has sent me before you to bring life."[15] In other words, Joseph now remembers his trauma as a force for good. In his new interpretation, he suffered precisely so others could live.

Joseph teaches us to embrace this third stage of healing, the stage of re-interpreting our memories. Forgetting the past can only take us so far before the trauma reasserts itself in painful and damaging ways. Ultimately, we must integrate our memories into a redemptive framework. To be truly fruitful, we must explain – to ourselves, if not to others – how our most traumatic moments, through God's strange grace, created some good.

Vayigash – It's All in the Name

In this week's reading, Jacob travels to Egypt to visit Joseph, his long-lost son. On the way, God appears to him and calls out "Jacob, Jacob." It's odd that God uses the name Jacob, and not Israel. God has twice changed Jacob's name to Israel, both times saying, "You shall no longer be called Jacob, but rather Israel shall be your name."[16] And, in fact, the biblical narrator uses the name Israel in describing how Jacob/Israel is about to leave Canaan. So why does God now use the name Jacob? For that matter, why, in our prayers, do we mostly refer to Jacob/Israel as Jacob? The *Amidah*

---

15. Ibid. 45:5.
16. Ibid. 32:29; 35:10.

(Judaism's long central prayer) speaks of the God of Jacob, not the God of Israel.

The name Israel means "God wrestler." Most commentators claim this refers to the Jewish vocation of arguing with God – in the tradition of Abraham arguing with God over the destruction of Sodom, or the Chasidic rabbi Levi Isaac of Berdichev symbolically trying God before a Jewish court. Levi Isaac, in fact, claims that, as the people of Israel, we fight against the very notion of inevitability. "God decrees," he writes, "and the righteous Jew struggles."

Now, throughout Jacob's life, he has been aware of God's prediction that his descendants will suffer slavery in Egypt. As Israel, he has resisted fulfilling this dreadful prophecy. First, he attempts to retire in Canaan. And even now, he makes it clear that he only intends a short visit to Egypt, not a move.

So God calls him "Jacob," (twice!) to teach him that it's time to stop resisting the inevitable. For better or for worse, it's Jacob's destiny to lead his people into Egypt, and eventual slavery. In other words, it's time for Jacob to stop being Israel – to stop fighting.

One of the biggest challenges in life is knowing when to be Israel, and when to be Jacob. Should we continue medical treatments – for ourselves or for our loved ones – or let nature take its course? Should we struggle to control our children's most important decisions, or learn to let go? As Jews, we often stand in the tension between Israel and Jacob, between fighting and relinquishing our control by placing our lives in God's hands.

Vayechi – Benevolent Forgiveness

This week we conclude the book of Genesis. I've always maintained that Genesis' most important theme is forgiveness. The final dialogue includes Joseph's extraordinary words of forgiveness, and his action here resolves four generations of sibling conflict.

But, to be more precise, this isn't merely forgiveness; it's a particular type of forgiveness. Joseph offers what I could call a "benevolent forgiveness" – a forgiveness that flows from a powerful person to someone less powerful. We get an early taste of this type of forgiveness several chapters before, when the more powerful Esau forgives Jacob, his less powerful brother. "Benevolent forgiveness" is when the forgiving party has both the motive and opportunity to wreak vengeance, but chooses instead to forgive. In Joseph's case he was certainly poised to extract the bitterest possible vengeance from his brothers, who threw him in a pit, and then sold him into slavery. Instead, he forgives.

I recently re-read one of my favorite Shakespeare plays, "A Midsummer Night's Dream." Without going into too much detail, I would claim that the theme here is also benevolent forgiveness. Shakespeare resolves his wacky plot first with the powerful King of the Fairies forgiving his less powerful wife, and then with Theseus, the King of Athens, forgiving one of his subjects. In the end, the fairy Pucks asks for forgiveness from the audience – certainly the most powerful force in the theater, with its ability to offer or withhold applause. Shakespeare seems to be saying that romantic love is frivolous and undependable, but benevolent forgiveness solves all problems.

But how can we possibly incorporate this idea into our lives? Most of us are not Josephs – tyrants, or kings or prime ministers – able to bestow forgiveness from on high. And even if we find ourselves in relatively powerful positions, a condescending forgiveness may in fact create added bitterness.

I would suggest that the trick here is not power, but perspective. Proper perspective allows us to stake out higher ground and forgive from a high place. For example, Joseph continually addresses his brothers not by their names, but using the word "brother." Here, he's announcing that he won't allow the one injury to define their relationship in its entirety. He sees the relationship in perspective – from the high ground – and finds much more than the one instance of hurt. Also, he continually invokes historical perspective, reminding the brothers of both their shared past and future destiny. Here, he reminds them that their broader universe is much bigger than their particular relationship. From this high place, Joseph sees that, regardless of his personal feelings, he needs to forgive his brothers so they can all get on with the business of building up the Jewish people.

Feuding families need to develop similar broad perspectives in order to forgive. For example, squabbling siblings can learn to look beyond specific injuries, and see the whole relationship. Or, a troubled husband and wife – even if they end up divorcing – can forgive each other, once they see that their world contains not just each other, but children, friends, communities. From that high place, they can learn to forgive for the sake of others – particularly the children. This is our form of "benevolent" forgiveness, flowing from the high places of generosity and perspective.

Chapter 2

EXODUS

Shemot – The Legacy of the Midwives

This week's reading contains one of the most intriguing chapters of the Exodus saga: the story of the midwives. Two elements of this story stand out for me. The first comes when Pharaoh complains that the midwives haven't followed their orders to kill the newborn male Israelites. The midwives respond that the Israelite women are "*chayot.*"[1]

The word "*chayot*" literally means animals, but the midwives can be understood here in two ways. On one level, they're excusing themselves to Pharoah by insulting the Israelite women. "These women are like animals," they're saying, "primitive and feral. Like animals, they give birth too quickly for us to intervene and kill the males."

But the word comes from the root "*chai,*" meaning life. So, on a deeper level, the midwives are telling Pharaoh that the Israelites are dynamic and lively – too filled with life for you to ever defeat. In fact, in a subtle but powerful way, the midwives here are contrasting ancient Egypt's famous cult of the dead with the Israelite culture of life. Death, they are saying, will never defeat life.

The other fascinating element is how the Midrash identifies

1.   Exodus 1:19.

Moses' sister Miriam as one of the two midwives. With this inge-
nious piece of exegesis, the rabbis transform Miriam into a true
heroine of life. In the Torah text, she's the one who rescues baby
Moses, and manages to get her mother hired as the infant's wet
nurse. The Midrash, in addition to identifying her as a midwife –
a facilitator of life – claims that she encouraged Israelite husbands
to have sex with their wives, despite the discouraging situation.
The rabbis also credit her with providing the life-giving water in
the desert. Altogether, she becomes the perfect representative of
the culture of life, opposed in every way to the Egyptian cult of
death.

Our important question that faces us today is: how should
Jews put the ideals of a culture of life into practice? One easy answer is to have more children. But this leads to a second, troubling
question. Yes, we're commanded to have lots of children, and the
Jewish people face a demographic crisis both here and in Israel.
On the other hand, overpopulation creates a serious, global, environmental, and health crisis. Is it morally tenable to say that other
people should stop having children but not us? I'm not sure I have
the answer to that question.

In any case, the midwives' story gives us another way of
looking at a culture of life. As a reward for rescuing Israelite babies, God gives the midwives "*batim*,"[2] which means "houses."
Many commentators interpret the word as meaning large families, which certainly fits the context and theme of the story. But
I would suggest that *batim* can also mean "households," or even
"communities."

For me, supporting a culture of life can mean enhancing the
quality of life, both for ourselves, and for non-Jews. And one of
the biggest global crises today is unstable families and communities. In fact, it's accurate to say that the problem today for many
people is not too few children, or too many children, but unstable
families, and unsteady communities – in other words, tottering

2.   Ibid. 1:21.

support systems, which lead to all sorts of poverty and violence. Jews today can best support a culture of life – and honor Miriam, our heroine – by supporting *batim* – households, families, communities.

Va'era – A Search for God

In contrast to the patriarchs, Abraham, Isaac, and Jacob, Moses often experiences God as a riddle, or a puzzle. When Moses first asks for God's name, God replies enigmatically, "I will be what I will be."[3] Later, God, for reasons no one can comprehend, tries to kill Moses.[4] This week's reading introduces yet another puzzle. God tells Moses that He appeared to Abraham, Isaac, and Jacob as "El Shaddai," but never revealed to them His true name (the Hebrew word YHVH). The problem is that this is simply not true. God often used the name YHVH in describing Himself to the patriarchs. Obviously, God isn't lying to Moses; in His own enigmatic way, He's telling Moses something altogether different. He's giving Moses another divine puzzle to solve.

Why all the riddles? Moses has a much more difficult job than the patriarchs. Abraham's job, to put it bluntly, is to leave home so that God can make him rich and famous. Moses, on the other hand, must confront the most powerful army in the world, led by Pharoah, the most stubborn person of all time. God tells Moses at the very outset that, at first, he'll fail. So, in order to fulfill his mission, Moses must search for buried spiritual resources, hidden sources of strength. God provokes Moses with puzzles, so he will deeply probe God's nature, and find those elements which can help him liberate his people.

---

3. Ibid. 3:14.
4. Ibid. 4:24–26 describes God trying to kill Moses. Tsipporah, Moses' wife, saves him at the last moment by flinging a foreskin at Moses' feet. Many commentators have tried to explain this uncanny story, with sometimes creative, but never really satisfying, results. My point here is that God sometimes behaves in baffling ways to Moses, engaging in wordplay and actions that defy explanation.

In the Zohar, Judaism's mystical masterpiece, two of God's names are "Who" and "What." In other words, God's very essence should provoke questions. When we are in crisis or pain, or face difficult tasks, asking questions about God launches us on an inner journey, where we search for hidden resources. The Zohar reminds us that sometimes, in our great despair, we cry out: "Who will heal me?" The Zohar replies that it's precisely "Who" that will heal us – God, whose name is "Who," in a hidden form. In our spiritual quest, provoked by divine questions, we can find the hidden places in our own God-given souls, untouched by pain. From there, we reach out, and begin to heal.

Bo – Asking the Right Question

Why does God harden Pharaoh's heart? Doesn't this conflict with our notion of free will? After all, if God places stubbornness directly into Pharoah's soul, how could he ever repent?

Many commentators have tackled this question, but God Himself answers it in this week's Torah reading. God says, "I've hardened Pharoah's heart and the hearts of his servants *in order to place my miracles before them*." Later, God says: "I've hardened Pharoah's heart *so that Egypt will know that I am God*." In other words, God interferes with Pharoah's free will – in fact, God performs all His redemptive miracles – in order to impress Egyptian culture.

This is odd, because we're used to thinking of the Exodus as a Jewish story with a specifically Jewish audience. But, in actual fact, by liberating the Israelite slaves, God creates a sacred myth not just for Jews, but for Egyptians. Every year we're commanded to tell the story; but Egypt is meant to tell the same story – just for different reasons.

We tell the story to remind ourselves that we're not slaves. Our story instills a love for freedom in our hearts. Egyptians should tell the story to remind themselves that they are no longer slave masters. The Exodus, hopefully, instills an abhorrence of economic exploitation in their souls.

Today, when we read this story, or when we celebrate Pass-over, it's important to look at the narrative from both perspectives. In contemporary America, American Jews in general are relatively prosperous, and therefore, in terms of class, are closer to the aristocracy – or slaveowners – than the poor. Jews today therefore share a greater socio-economic bond with the ancient Egyptian slave masters than with the destitute Israelite slaves. In many ways, we're closer to Pharaoh than to Moses.

So, it's certainly proper to ask ourselves this Passover, "Am I still a slave?" But we should also ask the Egyptian question: "Am I Pharoah?" Unless we ask ourselves both questions, we're missing half the story.

B'shalach – The Right Arguments

According to a wonderful Midrash, the Jews divided into four groups as the Egyptians pursued them at the Red Sea. One group advocated jumping into the sea; another suggested returning to Egypt; a third urged the Israelites to fight; and the fourth suggested they pray.

On the one hand, this sounds like Jewish factionalism – annoying, counterproductive, but unfortunately typical. I'm reminded of the old joke of two Jews on a desert island who found three synagogues: one for each, and one that neither will step foot in.

I would claim, however, that, in this case at least, the Israelites' behavior was completely appropriate. The most significant issue confronting the Jews of that time and place was Egypt. It's natural they should divide into factions. Factions allow us to articulate strategies when facing serious issues. If the groups, with God's help, maintain connections, each can learn from the others' positions.

In fact, the three major synagogue movements in America arose because of differences over how to face the most significant Jewish issue of the nineteenth century: modernity. As Jews left the ghetto, different strategies emerged. Reform (I'm simplifying, of course) suggested removing those Jewish practices which separated us from our new neighbors. The Conservative movement suggested conserving most of those practices, but to march full speed ahead away from the ghetto. Orthodoxy sensed the dangers and temptations of life outside the ghetto, and suggested doubling our efforts at preserving those distinctive Jewish practices (some, of course, suggested moving back into the ghetto). Each position, in my opinion, had its own integrity, validity, and place in American-Jewish life.

The problem is that modernity is no longer the most important issue facing our community. We left the ghetto over a hundred years ago, but we're left with institutions that were created to face this very old, and mostly outdated, dilemma. This, I believe, is why so many Jews today feel that none of the major synagogue movements speak to them in a way that is meaningful or relevant.

What are the major issues facing the Jewish community today? That's easy to answer. I'll offer just a few. How do we attract the vast number of uncaring Jews? Should we or should we not live in Israel? What is the religious/historical significance of the territories Israel occupied/liberated in 1967? Are we, or are we not, commanded by God to follow the *mitzvot* (Torah commandments)? Most interested Jews could list many more. However, because of our attachment to the old institutions, there aren't very many factions within American Judaism that have coalesced around any of these questions. The challenge for the next century is not to give up our famous factionalism. It's to form factions around issues that really matter.

Yitro: Learning and Growing

This week's reading is one of the few that is named after an individual, in this case Moses' father-in-law, Jethro. We don't know much about Jethro, but we can say definitively that he was a spiritual person. Before meeting Moses, he was a pagan priest. Later, like many religious giants in history, he experienced a profound spiritual transformation and embraced Judaism. What triggered this transformation? According to the Midrash, three distinct events influenced him: the Red Sea miracle, the battle with Amalek, and the Sinai revelation.

The Red Sea miracle and the Amalek battle represent the two poles of human emotional response. The Israelites responded to the miracle at the Sea with singing, joy, and celebration. They responded to Amalek with mourning, loss, and trauma. So, I might argue that in studying Judaism, Jethro found a spiritual system which easily incorporates both joy and sorrow – a religious culture which brings God into both our celebrations and our mourning. And that's what attracted him to Judaism.

But there's more. Jethro was also impressed by Sinai. For Jews, Sinai represents learning and growth. We learned the Torah at Sinai, but we also extrapolated a complex legal system from God's words. Because of Sinai, we continue to learn and grow. Putting all three events together, I would claim that Jethro discovered a spiritual system in which individuals have the capacity to learn and grow through joy and loss.

It's obviously easier to grow spiritually from joy. At weddings or bar/bat mitzvahs, our joy can propel us to greater moral commitments or stronger relationships with God. It's much harder to grow through loss. But Judaism does encourage us to take on new commitments when our loved ones die – in other words to grow through loss. And one of our most important commandments is to love the stranger[5] because we were once strangers – that is to transform our trauma into compassion, to become better human beings because of our sorrow.

When Jethro, a spiritual seeker, encountered Judaism, he discovered a religion that brings the divine into both our bleakest moments and our seasons of joy. But he also discovered people learning and growing through joy and sorrow. And that discovery changed his life.

---

5. Ibid. 22:20.

Mishpatim – Working with Integrity

This week's reading repeats a *mitzvah* we learned last week – the commandment to observe Shabbat. But in Mishpatim, the commandment is worded differently. Last week, as part of the Ten Commandments, the Torah instructed us to: "Remember the Sabbath Day.... Six days you shall do all your work..." This week, the Torah tells us: "You shall work six days, but on the seventh day you shall rest." In other words, last week's commandment begins with Shabbat, while this week's begins with the working week.

Many of us overlook the fact that God does not just command us to rest on Shabbat; God also commands us to work during the week. The different wordings reflect a different emphasis on the work week. The Ten Commandments suggest that Shabbat functions as a sort of spiritual big bang, infusing our work with holiness, and giving us strength as we wait for the next Shabbat. For the Ten Commandments, work is secondary to Shabbat. This week's reading, on the other hand, suggests that work comes first. Working well, with honesty and integrity, allows us to enjoy Shabbat. In fact, according to this interpretation, we only deserve Shabbat's joy if we work properly.

I prefer this second interpretation, which emphasizes work. The Ten Commandments needed to stress Shabbat because the whole Sinai experience represents our spiritual big bang; the Sinai revelation infuses all of history with holiness. But nowadays, in our prosaic world, many of us spend most of our waking moments at work. Our burden now is to work in such a way that we can truly savor the joy of Shabbat.

How can we work well, and with integrity? Interestingly, this week's reading is filled with work-related commandments. Many of the laws – such as keeping honest weights and measures – fit an American-style service economy, where professionals perform services for clients. The details differ depending on the situation, but, in general, the laws insist that we properly evaluate our full responsibility to our customers. If we honestly consider, and then fulfill, all of our obligations to those we serve, then we deserve the beauty and rest of Shabbat.

In today's complex, capitalistic economy, it is often difficult to focus on our relationships with customer/clients. Large corporations or stockholders demand our loyalty, often to the exclusion of those we serve. Within this challenging structure, we must, nevertheless, learn to fully appreciate the purity of the professional-client relationship, with all the nuances of mutual responsibilities. Then we can work well for six days and enjoy our Rest.

Terumah – The Power of Imagination

This week's reading marks the beginning of the Tabernacle construction project, an enterprise which stretches through four additional readings. Inevitably, a spirit of sadness accompanies us as we study these chapters. After all, we know that the Temples these readings describe – these centers of Jewish spiritual life – will twice be reduced to rubble. The Jewish people carry the tragedy of this loss throughout history. It invades even our wedding celebrations, which we conclude by breaking a glass in memory of the broken Sanctuaries. In Jewish spirituality, these shattered buildings symbolize our bloody history, our broken hearts, or our shattered and unhealed world.

An odd passage in the Talmud claims that we reproduce the experience of Temple worship by studying these Torah readings. This strikes me as an outrageous claim. How can the cerebral act of study compare to the gross physicality of slaughtering an animal on God's behalf? Really, though, this outrageous claim testifies to the power of the Jewish imagination. Studying the Temple blueprints creates a picture of a restored Temple in our minds. Broadly speaking, in our brokenness, we imagine a future filled with wholeness and healing. And, in fact, several of the *Haftarot* (readings from the Prophets, corresponding to the Torah section) connected with these readings feature Ezekiel's vision of a restored Temple. Ezekiel's Temple existed only in his head, but his imaginative musings helped comfort and heal the community of Jews that lived through the first destruction.

We often overlook the creative imagination as a powerful tool for healing. But Jews have always responded to catastrophes with imaginative visions of a better world. Our historic longing for Zion created the modern Zionist movement which allowed us, as a people, to survive the Holocaust. Similarly, when our hearts feel broken, the first step towards the light is often picturing a better tomorrow. Our imagination conjures a future of healing, and, somehow, God helps us turn this fiction into reality.

This may be the secret to Jewish survival. Despite a past filled with brokenness, we always imagine – envision – something better.

Tetzaveh – The Beauty of Creation

In studying the many chapters devoted to constructing the desert Tabernacle, the rabbis offered several metaphoric meanings for the *Mishkan*. In this week's reading, which begins with instructions for building the Eternal Light, the rabbis insisted that the entire project symbolizes the building of a human being, with the light symbolizing the soul.

Since human beings were responsible for creating the *Mishkan* (as opposed to the world, which God created), this metaphoric reading implies that human beings must create other human beings. The Torah commentator known as the Kli Yakar, in a beautiful comment, suggests that God told Moses to "create" other souls "from Moses' own essence…from Moses' extra portion of light, from his glory."[6] How do we, as human beings, create other souls, using our "own essence," or our own "extra portion of light?" Obviously mentors and teachers in some way "create" the souls of their students, just as friends influence other friends and lovers "create" new dimensions in their lovers' souls. But this metaphor most dramatically concerns parents who, more than anyone else, "create" the essential personalities of their children.

---

6. *Kli Yakar* to Exodus 27:20.

Rav Kook once wrote that every person has the ability both to create and destroy the entire world. I used to read this extraordinary comment on a grand scale, thinking of Auschwitz on the one hand, and the State of Israel on the other. As a species, we carry an astounding capacity for evil and good. But Rav Kook might easily have been referring to individual parents, who, using our extra portions of light, nurture children and create healthy, vibrant souls, but who also, potentially, inflict great harm. Rav Kook here reminds us of the awesome responsibility that comes with having children.

How, as parents, do we create and not destroy? My own parents "created" me by offering words of encouragement at my bleakest times. I remember, in particular, a letter I received from my late father at a crossroads in my life, where he reminded me that he would support any and all of my choices. He ended the letter with the words: "I bless you that you find love and fulfillment in whatever you choose."

I believe we best express our creative abilities – as parents, friends, or lovers – with words of blessing. God concluded the creation of the world with a blessing. This was neither an epilogue nor an anti-climax, but part and parcel of God's creative activity. We create each other when we offer words like "I believe in you," or "You're stronger than you think," or, in difficult times, "You'll get through this," or "I bless you." As parents, friends, lovers, and teachers, we demonstrate our "extra portions of light," "our glory," and our awesome creative powers, with our blessings.

Ki Tissa: Making a Home for God

We usually read the Golden Calf narrative as a story of sin and forgiveness. And, in fact, our Yom Kippur liturgy quotes passages from the story several times, including, most dramatically, at the end of the Kol Nidrei (Yom Kippur Evening) prayers. The dialectics of sin and forgiveness provide a useful lens for the story, giving us a powerful paradigm for repentance in our own lives.

But we can also read the incident as a story of absence, longing, and despair. The Israelites demand that Aaron build the calf because they feel the absence of Moses. Aviva Zornberg, a remarkable Torah educator, compares the people's emotions here to a baby longing for its mother. Later, the people mourn and wail when God tells them He will no longer guide them Himself, but, will send an angel instead. Moses actually becomes suicidal when he experiences the absence of God's "face."[7]

This story describes a genuine religious dilemma: the existential loneliness that arises from feeling God's absence. The Psalmist complains to God, "You hid your face from me; I became utterly confounded."[8] We all experience confounding moments in our lives when it feels like God has turned His back to us.

Jewish tradition discovered the concept of the *Shechinah* as an antidote to this profound loneliness. *Shechinah* literally means "God's indwelling." Before ordering the people to construct the Tabernacle, God instructs them: "Build me a sanctuary that I may live (*shachanti*) in you."[9] Jewish mysticism portrays the *Shechinah* as, among other things, the attribute of God that lives within us.

How do we bring the *Shechinah* down to us? In other words, how do we bridge the existential gap we sometimes feel between God and ourselves? By making, within ourselves, worthy homes for God – decent places for God to dwell. I can imagine three such places: our communities, our families, and our hearts. We need to ask ourselves: are the communities we've built places of gossip, hostility, and harmful language? If so, they are not worthy homes for God. But when we act with lovingkindess, generosity, and *Tikkun Olam*,[10] then we have built decent homes for God.

Similarly, cruelty and abuse in our families demean God's place in our homes, while love and compassion make a fitting place for the *Shechinah*. Hatred and bitterness pollute God's

---

7. Exodus 33:15.
8. Psalms 30:8.
9. Exodus 25:8.
10. *Tikkun Olam* is a Hebrew phrase which translates as, "repairing the world" or "perfecting the world." It is a central concept in Judaism.

dwelling, but generosity and wisdom enhance God's home in our hearts. We fill the emptiness caused by God's absence by cleaning up our own homes – our synagogues, our families, our souls. We make sanctuaries out of our most precious dwellings so that the *Shechinah* can live among us.

Vayakhel-Pekudei – Doing God's Work

This week's reading completes the instructions for building the Tabernacle. For the fifth time, the text interrupts these instructions with the commandment to rest on Shabbat, because God rested on the seventh day. Clearly, the Torah is comparing God's work in forming the world to our work in building the *Mishkan*. The Rabbis amplify this parallel with a beautiful Midrash, where every element in the *Mishkan*, from the planks, to the cloth, to the joints, to the Ark, directly corresponds to something in the natural world. It's as if, by building the *Mishkan*, we're creating a parallel world.

How can we understand the differences and similarities between these two worlds? According to Genesis, God created the natural world as a theater for human achievement. God commands the first humans to "fill the world and subdue it."[11] This physical world is the place for human work. The *Mishkan*, on the other hand, lies apart from the grand and sometimes petty, or even destructive, natural world of human achievement. The *Mishkan* is, in fact, the theater for God's work.

What, exactly, is God's work? There's a lovely story in the Talmud where two rabbis pass the ruins of the ancient Temple without emotion, but break down in tears upon seeing the ruins of a modest home. They explain that the home formerly served as a soup kitchen that fed hundreds of hungry people daily. That soup kitchen, more than the grand Temple, was a place for God's work.

Another Midrash deepens our understanding. This week's reading contains instructions for building the basin. In the

11. Genesis 1:28.

Midrash, all the Israelite women offer their mirrors as material for this basin. At first, Moses takes offense: we should build a part of the *Mishkan*, he asks, with objects of vanity? But God explains to Moses that the women used the mirrors as slaves in Egypt, in order to make themselves attractive to their husbands, thereby improving general morale, and inspiring the conception of more babies. Every time the women see the mirrored basin, God explains, they will remember the noblest parts of themselves.

God's work, in other words, is the tasks we perform that bring out the best in ourselves. And a true sanctuary is a mirror where, because of our spiritual work, we see the noblest, most generous parts of our souls – those parts that yearn to feed the hungry, to teach poor children to read, to comfort the ill and bereaved. A sanctuary is a holy mirror where we see ourselves doing God's work.

Chapter 3

LEVITICUS

Vayikra – Accountability

Chapter 4 of this week's reading contains an assortment of animal sacrifices that different types of people bring for sins that fall into the category of "*shogeg*." *Shogeg* is a difficult word to translate. Most render it as "inadvertent," but it really means a serious, almost negligent mistake, somewhere between a premeditated crime, which the Bible calls *ma'al*, and the Talmud later refers to as *mazid*, and a complete accident, which the Talmud terms *ahnus*. It's important to try to translate this word with some precision because most of the sins that most of us commit fall into the category of *shogeg*. They're not malicious crimes, but they're certainly not accidents.

Interestingly, the Torah presents a sliding financial scale of *shogeg* offerings. The High Priest offers the most expensive sacrifices, followed by the "people" as a whole, followed by an individual tribal leader, followed by the ordinary citizen, who offers the cheapest sacrifice, a lamb. Most commentators agree that the Torah here teaches that the sins of leaders are more serious than the sins of ordinary folk, since a leader's misdeeds often affect, and even implicate, everyone in the community. Nachmanides points out that bringing sacrifices is really a socially beneficial system, since it gives leaders the opportunity to publicly admit their mistakes, and gain forgiveness from both God and the people.

Nowadays, of course, political leaders are extremely reluctant to admit their mistakes. In presidential elections, most candidates run as fast as they can away from admitting errors, even though it's obvious to everyone that every national politician makes mistakes. So why is it so difficult for today's leaders to publicly acknowledge these mistakes?

This is, of course, a difficult question, tied up with the complexities of our democratic political system. But our reading offers two hints that we could try to incorporate into our own lives, if not our own political culture. The tribal leader offers the *shogeg* sacrifice because "he was informed" of his sin (Heb. "*hoda alav*"). Who informed him? Ancient Israelite kings relied on prophets whose express job was to inform them when they had sinned. David's prophet Nathan acted with great courage when he accused David of murder and adultery. These prophets acted as fully independent moral critics, who enjoyed great spiritual authority. In our country today, there are very few fully independent religious voices offering moral critiques of our leaders.

The Torah also guarantees the leader that, after admitting his sin and offering the sacrifices, "he will be forgiven." Ancient leaders had every expectation that they could achieve closure on difficult issues, as long as they were sincere in their acceptance of responsibility, and expressed contrition. Our current political/legal system offers few guarantees of closure, and investigations drag on for years.

So at least part of our problems with leaders is systemic. We have no independent religious critics, and no guaranteed closure. This is just one example of how contemporary society can learn from Torah.

Tsav – Beyond Freedom and Slavery

We usually associate *chametz* and *matza* (leavened and unleavened bread) with Passover, when we eat the latter, and avoid the former, in order to relive our ancestors' journey from slavery to freedom. But the Torah occasionally mentions both *chametz* and *matza* outside the context of Passover. For example, in this week's pre-Passover reading, the Torah instructs us to eat *matza* and avoid *chametz* when offering both the guilt and sin sacrifices. Here, these two food products clearly symbolize something beyond freedom and slavery, something that, for *matza* encourages atonement, and for *chametz* discourages it. In fact, the Jewish tradition offers at least three symbolic references for *chametz* and *matza* beyond the issues of slavery and freedom.

Rabbi Alexandri, in the Talmud, suggests that *chametz* symbolizes arrogance – the "yeast in the dough" which puffs up our egos. Arrogance obviously prevents true repentance, since, without humility, we can never recognize our own sins, or God's authority to judge us.

The Gerrer Rebbe teaches that *matza* represents noble speech, since it provokes us, on Passover, to tell a holy story. *Chametz*, therefore, symbolizes harmful speech, like gossip or slander. According to the Gerrer Rebbe, we can't fully atone for our sins until we purify our speech.

Finally, the Kli Yakar associates *chametz* with the "evil inclination," which he defines as the sex drive, or, more broadly, the human urge to conquer and achieve. Normally, of course, we need this inclination in order to attain a fully integrated human soul (and to propagate). But there are times, particularly when we are atoning for sin, when we need to fight our sometimes destructive ambitions. *Matza*, according to the Kli Yakar, symbolizes this fight.

These metaphors add symbolic resonance to our Passover housecleaning. While scrubbing our kitchens and stoves, we are not just physically eliminating the *chametz* from our houses. We're embarking on a crucial spiritual quest to root out arrogance, harmful language, and destructive ambitions from our souls. The most obvious journey on Passover is toward freedom. But, as we eat *matza* and forego *chametz*, we also strive to create a pure heart and a humble soul.

Shemini – A Culture of Rage

This week's reading contains the baffling story of Nadav and Avihu, Aaron's sons, whom God immolates because they offered a "strange fire," which God "did not command."[1] It's impossible to fully understand the implication of this brutal story, but we can begin to uncover some lessons by focusing on the Hebrew word *ketzef.* Shortly after Nadav and Avihu's deaths, Moses worries that God's "*ketzef*" will erupt "against the entire congregation."[2] We usually translate *ketzef* as "anger," but, in this case, it's hard to see why God would become angry at all Israelites because of the deeds of two boys (it's hard enough to understand why God erupted in anger against the two boys).

Ketzef here obviously means a fiery, uncontrollable rage – a force that transcends rationality. In fact, the Torah often uses *ketzef,* usually in the book of Numbers, to refer to God's destructive, seemingly irrational, rage. Interestingly, in our reading, the Torah describes Moses as feeling *ketzef* after Nadav and Avihu's deaths, when he discovers that Aaron and his surviving sons did not properly perform a sacrifice. Moses, in other words, feels enraged, and ready to burst out beyond rational control.

If this story, then, is about rage, Aaron emerges as the hero. When Moses informs Aaron of his son's deaths, in the process implying that the boys may be to blame, the Torah tells us that "Aaron was silent (*Vayidom Aharon*)."[3] Aaron might well have lashed out against both Moses and God, but he holds his peace. In other words, in a rage-filled environment, where Aaron has every right to respond with rage, he exercises self-control.

It has long been my feeling that we live in a culture of rage. This rage is expressed in increasingly violent movies; by radio talk show hosts, who use anger as their principle mode of communication; and in the Western world's highest rate of violent crime,

---

1. Leviticus 10:1.
2. Ibid. 10:6.
3. Ibid. 10:3.

especially among teenagers. A friend once told me he suspects that one of the reasons for the enormous popularity of Mel Gibson's "The Passion of Christ" is because its hammering violence perfectly captures the zeitgeist of popular American culture.

In a culture consumed with rage, our obligation is to follow Aaron's example and control ourselves. Anger is a normal human emotion, which we cannot and should not obliterate from our psyches. But we can, and should, prevent normal anger from bursting into rage. We can fight the *ketzef* in our own lives by following the advice of our sage, Hillel who wrote, "Be like the students of Aaron, loving peace and pursuing peace."

Tazriah – The Sanctity of the Human Body

This week's reading offers laws of childbirth and leprosy. This seems like an odd combination, but a question by the kabbalistic commentator Ohr HaChayim clarifies the similarity of these two subjects. Why, the Ohr HaChayim asks, does the Torah begin the portion with the words *"Ki Tazriah ve'yaldah,"* meaning "When a woman bears seed and gives birth"? Why do we need the extra phrase "bears seed" (*tazriah*), when "gives birth" would suffice?

First, it's important to note that the word *tazriah*, in traditional Hebrew, doesn't only mean "bears seed"; it's also the word for orgasm. So the Ohr HaChayim teaches us that this verse describes three female physical processes: 1. releasing an egg; 2. orgasm; and 3. childbirth. The next part of the verse adds two more: 4. continued bleeding; and 5. recovery. The next verse discusses yet another biological process: being born; though now the subject is the new baby rather than the mother. Altogether, the first two verses comment on six biological processes.

In fact, one of the major purposes of the book of Leviticus is to teach us to sanctify milestones in the life of the body. These biological milestones include happy ones, like budding sexuality and childbirth, and difficult ones, like illness (symbolized by leprosy) and death. We sanctify these bodily transitions with various rituals that remind us that the body is perhaps the most prominent evidence of God's love. Even when it is breaking down, the body remains God's greatest gift, because it's only through the body that we experience anything.

Our bodies' changes often mystify and even frighten us. Adolescence brings bleeding and skin eruptions; pregnancy transforms a woman in countless startling ways; illnesses such as leprosy bring weird and unpleasant changes; and aging causes gray hair and bad backs. Rituals marking all these changes bring God into our lives precisely when we feel most vulnerable and afraid.

A hospice nurse recently commented on NPR that helping a loved one die by sitting at the bedside, praying, and waiting is every bit as loving and intimate experience as watching a wife give birth. Death, in other words, is another milestone in the life of the body, another opportunity to invoke God's presence. We thank God for giving us bodies; for helping us through our bodies' early changes; for giving women the power to bring new bodies into the world. And we continue to thank God for the great gift of the body, even as it breaks down, and we return it to God before moving on to whatever comes next.

Metzorah – Standing Before God

This week's reading continues discussing certain conditions which make human beings impure (*tamei*). Interestingly, in Parashat Shemini, the Torah discussed pure and impure animals. Rashi comments that "just as in creation, animals preceded human beings, so in purity teachings do animals precede human beings."

With this comment, Rashi hints that human beings should be careful in proclaiming their superiority over animals. The Midrash, in fact, suggests that, should a person become arrogant, we should remind him or her that "[in creation] a worm came before you."[4] A prayer from the Yom Kippur service claims that "the difference between human beings and animals is nothing." That's a truly astonishing statement, until we read the first line of the next

---

4. Leviticus Rabbah 14:1.

prayer: "but we stand before God." In other words, according to this prayer, the only significant difference between humans and animals is our ability to "stand before God" – to develop an intimate relationship with God.

This idea explains the role of the priest in responding to a leper. At first glance, it seems strange that the Torah instructs a person afflicted with leprosy to first call a priest. A doctor would be a more likely choice; and, in fact, the priest does nothing to remove or cure the leprosy. The priest's role, however, is not to physically heal the leprosy (even in ancient times doctors existed for that purpose), but to reestablish the ill person's relationship with God.

Most of the impurities the Bible mentions in this section have the effect of alienating a person from God. Illness, death, family crises, sin – all these problems can potentially embitter our relationship with God, and even make us doubt His constant presence in our lives. We become like animals, unable to "stand before God." Certainly, under these circumstances, we should contact doctors, lawyers, social workers, or any other professionals who can help us during our physical crises. But, perhaps our first priority is to regain our human vocation by calling someone who can help us bring God back into our lives.

Strangely, these Torah readings – ancient and obscure – clarify the role of modern clergy. Human beings distinguish themselves from animals by reaching out to God. But sometimes plagues, both physical and psychological, block the path to God. It is the role of modern spiritual leaders to help us clear the way.

Acharei Mot-Kedoshim – Mourning and Questions

This week's reading begins with the words, "God spoke to Moses after the death of Aaron's sons who died in coming close to God." The death of Aaron's sons has always been a mystery, but this formulation makes these deaths seem utterly incomprehensible: why would anyone die "in coming close to God?" In fact, it's the very incomprehensibility of Aaron's loss that explains his first reaction:

silence. After Moses offers some strange comforting words, the Torah tells us "*Vayidom Aharon*," "Aaron was silent."

In his wisdom, Aaron realized that it's not healthy to ask questions during times of raw mourning. Certainly Aaron would want to know why his precious children died. And he had every right to ask. But during our deepest grief, silence plants the seeds of healing better than questions or protests. We actually include silence as part of our mourning rituals. When visiting a mourner during the traditional seven-day period of mourning, we're not supposed to speak unless the mourner initiates conversation. Jewish law recognizes that sometimes pure silence offers more comfort than words.

I recently returned from Israel where, on Holocaust Memorial Day at 10 AM, and *Yom Hazikaron* (the memorial day for victims of Israel's battles) at 11 AM, the entire country stands in silence, while listening to a screaming siren. These are powerful moments, since the siren seems to recreate the fresh, pure agony of loss, while the country responds mutely. Raging loss cannot be comforted by protests or questions, at least not initially. Raging loss requires silence.

Aaron's story also teaches us that, even in our deepest grief, we retain some emotional control. It certainly would have been natural and understandable for Aaron to rage against God and Moses. But he was wise enough to control his words, and thereby control his anger. Jewish mourning laws also demonstrate our ability to control emotions, even in our deepest sorrow. The *shiva* period, where we mourn for seven days in our home, allows us to feel the full force of our loss, but *shiva* is interrupted by Shabbat or a holiday. During our week of deepest mourning, we're required to turn on a dime emotionally. We mourn during the week, but on Shabbat we're not allowed to mourn. In fact, we're required to celebrate.

I also witnessed this emotional control in Israel. *Yom Hazikaron* comes exactly one day before *Yom Ha'atzmaut* – Israel's independence day, a day of joy and celebration. After twenty-four hours – actually, in the sixty seconds separating *Yom Hazikaron* from *Yom Ha'atzmaut* – Israelis turn on a dime, and go from profound sadness to joy.

My colleague Rabbi Jeffrey Wohlegellenter pointed out to me that this emotional control won't work unless the mourner is truly committed to the celebration. For mourners, it's the holiday itself (Shabbat or a festival) which replaces the healing powers of *shiva*. Those healing powers won't work at all unless we truly embrace the holy day. I would add that it's actually a supportive community which replaces the *shiva*. We celebrate Shabbat and festivals (and, of course, *Yom Ha'atzmaut*) with our community. Our friends – by singing, eating, and celebrating together – supplement the *shiva's* healing power.

One lesson from all this is to make sure we connect ourselves to a community. It becomes the very basis of healing from loss. We also learn that, as members of a community, we provide an essential component in healing a mourner. Our fellowship with mourners provides as much, if not more, healing than other mourning rituals. In other words, silence begins the healing, but community completes it.

Emor – Family Values

Even a casual observer of American politics would notice that the concept of "family" has become a political issue. Powerful groups now use our political system to promote legislation they think benefits "the family." These groups often focus on what they perceive as threats to the family, mostly external threats, including a lewd and violent popular culture, and, more recently, gay marriage.

What is "family?" The pro-family movement usually defines it, at least in its ideal state, as the classic nuclear unit – father, mother, children. Ironically, since the pro-family movement is religious, the Bible never embraces this definition. Many biblical families were polygamous. Biblical families were really clans – extended families that included uncles, aunts, and cousins, as well as slaves and concubines.

This week's reading offers a wonderful (and, I must say, a particularly Jewish) definition of family. According to Leviticus, when a priestly daughter marries out of the family, she can no longer eat the family food. If she later rejoins the family, through divorce or widowhood, then she can resume eating the family food. In other words, a family constitutes the people you eat with on a regular basis.

According to the Bible, then, what is the biggest threat to family? Superficially (but importantly), we threaten our families when we don't find time to share meals regularly.

More deeply, the biggest threat to biblical families is clearly jealousy. Cain's jealousy toward his brother destroys his family; Esau and Jacob's mutual jealousy breaks up their family; Joseph's brothers nearly kill Joseph because of their raging jealousy.

In other words, the Bible teaches us that threats to the family reside in our own hearts, and are not coming from external forces. Anger, bitterness, and petty jealousy are the destructive emotions that threaten our families. Of course, some external forces pose threats, including our culture and, frankly, parts of our socio-economic system. But looking outside of ourselves for the problems that plague our families leads to scapegoating, which is a close cousin to bigotry. Gay marriage, whatever else one might think of it, doesn't threaten the family. We're better off looking for those threats in our own hearts and in our own behavior.

Behar-Bechukatai – A Vision of Peace

This week's reading offers several visions of peace. The first promises a time when "the sword will not pass through the land."[5] For the Midrash, this means complete civil peace, where the Jewish people work together harmoniously. Another prophesies a condition where the Israelites will "chase your enemies, and they will fall before you by the sword."[6] This is the peace of the victor, where

5. Leviticus 26:6.
6. Ibid. 26:8.

we achieve peace by defeating and then intimidating all enemies – a peace of self-defense, but also, frankly an imposed peace, a Pax Romana (or Darth Vader's peace). Not mentioned, but lurking in the background, is another vision, this one offered by the prophet Isaiah, where "nation will not lift up sword against nation, nor learn war anymore."[7] This vision implies a fundamental shift in consciousness, where we learn to settle disputes peacefully.

Which is the superior vision? Obviously self-defense is important in this world, but Isaiah teaches us always to maintain the goal of shifting our consciousness away from war.

But our reading offers yet another vision of peace: a time when God will "expel aggressive animals from the land."[8] Most commentators see this as promising harmony between human beings and nature. Nachmanides points out that in Eden, wild animals and human beings lived in peace. It was only after the sin and expulsion, that animals, and other elements in nature, became actively hostile to human beings. Our reading, then, offers not just a vision of peace between nations (or peace between Jews), but also between human beings and the natural world.

As it happens, history now presents us with an opportunity to combine these two lofty visions. Most environmental scientists believe that the biggest threat from nature nowadays is global warming, a phenomena which could cause massive flooding, famine, and disease. Fortunately, many countries are now working together to manage this scourge. These countries (the United States is only peripherally involved), for the moment, are not lifting swords up against each other; they're not studying war, they're studying the environment, and are cooperating on a serious issue.

The fact is that for much of human history, we've pursued the "peace of the victor" with nature – fighting nature's powers with a constantly expanding industrial/technological civilization. Our

---

7. Isaiah 2:4.
8. Leviticus 26:6.

challenge now as human beings is to harmonize our relationship with nature, and as a blessed consequence stumble toward peace with each other.

Chapter 4

NUMBERS

Bamidbar – Count Them

In a famous biblical scene, God tells Abraham that his descendants will be as uncountable as the stars in the desert sky, or the grains of sand on the beach. Nevertheless, in this week's reading, God counts Abraham's descendants. Rashi explains that although human beings are incapable of physically counting the vast Jewish people, God can do it "because of love."[1] For Rashi, counting is an act of intimacy, where God acknowledges each and every one of the hundreds of thousands of individuals who make up the desert community of Israelites.

In other words, for human beings, large numbers dehumanize. The number 6 million conveys the enormity of the Holocaust, but it robs each victim of his or her unique individuality. I recently visited Ground Zero in lower Manhattan. The raw number of casualties (almost 4,000) left me cold, but the photographs of the victims touched me in ways no number ever could.

A poem by the brilliant Israeli poet Yehuda Amichai articulates the great human challenge of seeing past the numbers. "Count them all," he writes, consciously playing on God's challenge to Abraham, "for they are not like the grains of sand, so many, so

---

1. Rashi on Numbers 1:2.

small…Amid hovels, they contemplate the heavens." Here, Amichai urges us to appreciate the dignity, worth, complexity, and tragic beauty of every individual. Like Rashi, Amichai sees counting as an act of love, a way to counter the dehumanizing tyranny of numbers. Our challenge is to "count" everyone we see in the course of a busy day, to understand that each of us has a unique story, an individual manner of contemplating the heavens "amid hovels."

The Ishbitzer Rebbe, commenting on this week's reading, suggests we begin this activity by finding the unique gift that each of us, as individuals, brings to the Jewish people; not as cogs in a machine, but as creative and vital contributors to a great destiny. Once we discover our own individual missions, we'll better understand how every individual on Earth contributes unique gifts. We'll begin to imitate God by "counting" every one "because of love."

Naso – Looking Beyond the Surface

This week's reading includes a bizarre and frankly offensive ritual where a woman suspected of adultery drinks a mixture of water and dust in order to determine her guilt. In detailing the many steps a husband must take in order to bring his wife to trial, the Torah offers a complicated verse that not only sheds light on adultery, but also offers a window into the rabbinic mind.

The verse is Numbers 5:14: "A spirit of jealousy passes through [the husband] and he becomes jealous of her and she is impure; or a spirit of jealousy passes through him, and he becomes jealous of her and she is not impure." In the verse, the husband has his suspicions, but there are two possible sets of facts: she's either guilty, in which case his jealousy is justified, or she's not, in which case the problem is not her infidelity but his mistrust.

The Talmud uses this verse to teach that there are two ways of looking at a troubled marriage. Infidelity may be a problem, but jealousy may be as serious a challenge. In fact, jealousy can sometimes lead to infidelity. For the rabbis, there were always at least two ways of looking at any situation. They insisted on looking past the surface meaning of any issue, and discovering other possible interpretations.

As it happens, there are two possible ways to respond to infidelity in a marriage. The first obvious response is to dissolve the marriage and punish the perpetrator. That would certainly be the first reaction for most of us, were we faced with an unfaithful spouse. However, on deeper reflection, there is an alternative path. We can begin the difficult task of repairing the broken marriage, and work toward healing and reconciliation. We can look at the marriage as a whole, analyze how it broke down, and resolve to make changes.

The rabbinic tendency to see things both ways is, as we see, not just an intellectual game. It's a philosophy of life that teaches us to look beyond the easiest, most obvious, responses to our many dilemmas. Rabbinic thinking, in other words, shows us to absorb the awful consequence of sin, but then embrace the possibilities for hope and forgiveness.

B'ha'alotecha – Gathering In

In this week's reading, Aaron and Miriam complain about Moses "on account of his Kushite wife."[2] What, exactly, is their complaint? According to Rashi, they're not concerned with race or intermarriage. Instead, they object to the fact that Moses has chosen to remain celibate during his marriage. (Judaism doesn't encourage celibacy, so Aaron and Miriam conclude that Moses is simply taking on an additional spiritual burden, something that is unexpected of anyone else.) In other words, Moses' brother and sister are accusing him of a kind of spiritual snobbism – of raising himself above the community by living an overly ascetic life.

If that's their true complaint, then they've certainly misunderstood him. The Torah text itself interjects right away to remind us that, far from being a snob, Moses was "the most humble"

2. Numbers 12:1.

person of all time. And the two stories immediately preceding this episode testify to how desperately Moses does not want to exist apart from his community. During the episode of the quail, Moses pleads with God to remove him from his leadership position. And when two ordinary Israelites, Eldad and Medad, begin acting like prophets (in other words, acting like Moses), Moses rejoices and wishes that everyone would become prophets, like him. The last thing Moses desires is to set himself apart from the people, certainly not from his own brother and sister.

One word connects all these stories, and provides us with a particularly meaningful contemporary lesson. The word is *asaph*, meaning "gather in." After God punishes Miriam for slandering Moses, and sends her out of the camp, the entire community "gathers her in."[3] Earlier, at the height of Moses' lonely existential crisis, when, despite his best efforts, he feels apart from the community, the Torah tells us that the Israelites "gathered him in." In earlier readings, we find the word connected to leprosy. Lepers must leave the camp, but after their healing, the community "gathers them in." Remember, our tradition often interpreted lepers broadly to mean those living on the margins of the community – the poor, sick, or brokenhearted. Following this interpretation, the Torah commands those in the mainstream to look towards folks at the margins and "gather them in."

Obviously, this is a lesson whose time has come for contemporary American Judaism. Nowadays, there are more Jews who think of themselves as on the margins than in the mainstream. For whatever reason, poor Jews, singles, homosexuals, intermarrieds, divorced, and often widows and widowers, find themselves on the margins of Jewish life – disaffected and ultimately unaffiliated. Our challenge (and privilege), now, more than ever, is to institutionalize the concept of *asaph* – to reach out to the lonely and lost in our community, those on the outside of the camp, and gather them in.

3.   Ibid. 12:15.

Shelach – Touring Versus Settling

This week's reading includes the final paragraph of the *Shema* (the fundamental Jewish prayer which we are obligated to recite each day, in the evening and in the morning), and therefore introduces us to the central puzzle of this important prayer. The final paragraph urges us not to be led astray (*"lo taturu"*) by our hearts. But the first paragraph commands us to love God with all our hearts. So, are we supposed to follow our hearts and love God, or be wary of our hearts?

The answer lies in the Hebrew word *tur*, which literally means "wander," but which can also indicate a shallow, superficial engagement, similar to the English word "tour." The final paragraph warns us that cheap infatuation can lead us astray. On the other hand, sincere, sustained engagement leads us to authentic love – a love we can easily trust.

The biblical "Spy Story," which also appears in this week's reading, deepens our understanding of the Hebrew root *taturu*. In this story, the difficult puzzle is: How did things spin out of control so badly? Initially, the spies reported soberly on the land, accurately describing its people and geography. But after one of the spies, Caleb, interjects emotionally, the rest of the group starts exaggerating dramatically, calling the land a place that "eats its inhabitants,"[4] a land of giants, where the Israelites felt like grasshoppers. Why did most of the spies suddenly turn against the land?

Again, let's focus on the word *tur*. The Torah reports several times that the spies went out to wander around (*"la'tur"*) the land. Obviously, they were not fully committed to Israel. They came as tourists, not settlers. They were infatuated, but they weren't in love.

Judaism is a spiritual system that calls on us to avoid superficial engagements. This is true regarding a host of issues. The Talmud spends an inordinate amount of time discussing the details

4. Ibid. 13:32.

of certain cases in order to force us to think issues through with great care. From the Talmud's perspective, important social issues like responsibility for damages, or abortion, or medical ethics, require wisdom, and you can't become wise without serious intellectual and emotional commitment. Judaism calls on us to become wise.

In particular, we should always avoid the example of the spies. No Jew should be a "tourist" in the Land of Israel. When we visit Israel, or even read about it in the newspaper, we should strive for a full and authentic engagement. We should learn all we can about the Jewish state – the positive and the negative – and contemplate this information with great rigor. Otherwise we may reach the level of infatuation (*tur*), but we'll never really fall in love.

Korach – Arguing for the Sake of Heaven

This week's reading features Korach's rebellion against Moses. The rabbinic work Ethics of the Fathers offers the Korach/Moses dispute as an example of an argument that is "not for the sake of heaven," and therefore one that is doomed "not to endure."[5] But, in fact, there's an authentic spiritual issue separating Moses and Korach. Korach insists to Moses that "all the people are holy."[6] He sees radical equality in the community, with no separation of roles, no hierarchies. Moses, on the other hand, places great emphasis on both hierarchies and separation of roles. He designates the Levites as clergy and assigns each tribe and each individual a distinct role in the community. This particular dispute – egalitarianism versus hierarchical authoritarianism – actually does "endure" in Jewish history, with new disputants arising every century, up until our present day.

That being the case, what, then, is illegitimate about Moses' and Korach's argument? How is their dispute "not for the sake of heaven"? Rashi suggests that personal jealousies motivated Ko-

---

5. Ethics of the Fathers 5:17.
6. Numbers 16:3.

rach and his followers. Korach, according to Rashi, craved a higher priestly position than he received, and that alone, not greater principle, energized his rebellion. Bartenura, the great explicator of Ethics of the Fathers,[7] suggests that Korach was interested in "winning," not discovering a better way of governing. Other commentaries point out that Korach's methods of argument were illegitimate. He falsely accuses Moses of arrogance, an outrageous libel considering that the Torah calls Moses the most humble person of all time.

I might also add that Moses is not entirely free of blame. He mischaracterizes Korach's complaint, protesting to God that he never once took a bribe. But Korach never accuses Moses of corruption.

In other words, it's the seedy darkness of the human soul that pollutes this argument – the jealousies, ambitions, lies, and anger that color so many of our human interactions. The Vilna Gaon, a great mystic, though an opponent of Hasidism, teaches that in the higher Kabbalistic worlds, all disputes are "for the sake of heaven." But in the lowest world, the world of "action," the muck of human bias transforms idealistic disputes into wars and rivalries. Obviously, it's impossible to avoid this muck altogether. But many great mystics teach that human beings are the only creatures that have the ability to live simultaneously in the higher and lower worlds. We have the ability, in other words, to rise above our own petty ambitions, and argue "for the sake of heaven."

Chukat – From Death to Life

This week's reading features a shockingly moving scene, where Moses, at God's command, leads Aaron up to Mount Hor; strips off his brother's priestly garb; places the clothing on Aaron's sons; then watches his brother die. This scene reflects the themes of continuity, change, and, most powerfully, renewal – the movement from death to life.

---

7.   Bartenura to Ethics of the Fathers 5:17.

The entire reading, in fact, expresses these themes. We begin with the "red heifer" ritual which cleanses a person after contact with a corpse, and then continue quickly to the death of Miriam and Aaron. In other words, we begin with death. But the reading ends at the river Jordan, with images of flowing wells. In biblical times, water was a potent symbol of life. So the reading moves from death to life.

Similarly, early in the reading, the people complain because there's no water. But by the end they are, literally, singing by a well. Also, in the beginning, the people face a depressing military defeat at the hand of the Edomites. By the end, though, they have confidently defeated the Bashanites and the Amorites, and are poised to conquer the entire land of Canaan. The trajectory of the reading, then, is from death, defeat, dryness, and complaint to life, victory, and singing.

There is a counterintuitive sense to this narrative. We are used to thinking of life stories going from birth to death, or the story of a day taking us from morning to night. But our reading reverses the direction: we go from death to life; from darkness to light. Our *parashah* follows the order of the famous lines from Ecclesiastes: "a time to mourn and time to dance…a time to weep and a time to laugh."[8] Dancing follows mourning; laughter follows tears.

As individuals, our challenge is to internalize this order. When we mourn for those we love, or find ourselves mired in darkness for whatever reason, we must remember that life's trajectory takes us from mourning to dancing, from darkness to light. In fact, loss and illness can often provoke change in our lives, when we embrace life with a renewed sense of love and purpose. Mourning, through God's grace, carries the seed of healing within it, so, in the fullness of time, death becomes life; tears become laughter.

8. Ecclesiastes 3:4.

Balak – Foe Becoming Friend

This week's reading contains some of the most well-known sayings in Jewish literature, including "A nation that dwells apart (*Ahm levado yishkon*)"[9]; "There is no sorcery in Israel (*Lo kesem b'yisra'el*)"[10]; and, most famously, "How goodly are your tents, oh Jacob (*Mah tovu ohaleichah ya'akov*),[11] which we recite every morning upon entering the synagogue. Ironically, all of these poetic exclamations come from the non-Jewish prophet Balaam, a man the Midrash consistently characterizes as wicked. It's as if Balaam, normally an enemy, becomes a friend. At least for a moment.

Actually, an enemy momentarily becoming a friend is the great theme of our reading. The Moabite king Balak hires Balaam to curse the Israelites – to inflict harm with his words. Balaam tries several times, but God literally puts different words in his mouth. Balaam wants to wound his enemy – the Israelites. But he can't. God won't let him.

But all of a sudden, Balaam feels a shift in consciousness. The Torah tells us that he "lifted…his eyes and saw Israel dwelling in its tribes."[12] That's when he exclaims "How goodly are your tents, oh Jacob (*Mah tovu ohaleichah ya'akov*)." For once, these are not God's words, forced into Balaam's mouth, but Balaam's own authentic sentiments. From his hilltop, he looks at an enemy, but instead sees something else, something beautiful, something human – a friend. Rashi suggests that he saw how modestly the Israelites lived, and that moved him. Or Balaam may have simply experienced a moment of empathy as he observed men, women, and children, feeling a common humanity with the Israelites. Regardless of how we might define the experience, it's a moment of profound poetry amidst the weary prose of enmity.

9.   Numbers 23:9.
10. Ibid. 23:23.
11. Ibid. 24:5
12. Ibid. 24:2.

Jewish tradition has always offered dialectically opposed moods concerning enemies. On the one hand, the Torah urges us to "Remember (*zachor*)" the treachery of enemies such as Amalek. This is a sober mood, where we realistically assess those who may harm us. On the other hand, Balaam reminds us that we have the capacity of transcending feelings of enmity. For a moment, at least, an enemy can become a friend.

What if the evil Dr. Mengele had opened himself up to *Mah Tovu* moments when facing thousands of children? He might have seen human beings – sons and daughters – and not subhuman enemies. In fact, over the years, several ostensible suicide bombers have turned away from their homicidal missions when they saw innocent faces at pizza parlors, or bus stops, and not enemies. I myself have had moments when I visited Palestinian refugee camps, and I observed children playing, and families struggling to make a living, and I came to the realization that most Palestinians are not my enemies.

Certainly, we must engage in the sober task of *zachor* – remembering. We do have enemies and we have to deal with them. But everyday in our prayers we chant *mah tovu* – the words of Balaam. It's this poetry that alters our consciousness and reminds us that beneath the surface of the enemy is someone else, a human soul, and possibly a friend.

Pinchas – Ego-Driven Fanaticism

You'll forgive me if I get personal for a moment, but Pinchas is my Hebrew name, so I've been aware of his story ever since I can remember. And it's not exactly a pretty story – Pinchas slaughters an Israelite man and a Midianite woman with one spear thrust. In this week's reading, God praises him for this act, crediting him with averting God's presumably more violent wrath, and giving him, of all things, God's "covenant of peace."[13] Rashi, quoting the Talmud, adds color to Pinchas' character by suggesting that he was

---

13. Ibid. 25:12.

the type of fanatic (there's no other word) who was ridiculed by his society, but nevertheless stuck to his guns (or, actually, in this case, his spear). Rashi also makes him out to be even more zealously righteous than God, quoting God as saying, "he exploded with the rage (*ketsef*) that I should have exploded with."[14] My question is: Can I find anything admirable in my namesake? Is he, in some way, my secret role model?

I might be able to consider a positive response when I think of the context. Our reading highlights the transition taking place among Israelites. God instructs Moses to publicly bless Joshua as his successor because it's time for Moses to climb the mountain, look over it, and then die. Pinchas, Aaron's grandson, is of the new generation of Israelites – part of a self-confident breed, untainted by the notorious slave mentality. The new land and new culture will need brave fanatics, just as pre-state Palestine needed young zealots, unburdened by the trauma of Jewish history.

But no, even considering the context, I can't imagine myself emulating Pinchas, and killing two people out of righteous anger. The closest I can come – and even this is a stretch – is to imagine myself admiring someone *like* Pinchas – a true believer, who fights for what he thinks is right. But even here, the fanatics I have genuinely admired over the years – Theodore Herzl, Martin Luther King Jr., Ghandi, Rav Kook – would never pick up a weapon and kill someone in cold blood, even in support of their righteous causes. I have to admit that, namesake or not, Pinchas, for me, is closer to a terrorist than a hero – a true believer for sure, but fatally misguided.

But I can't leave it at that. It's my Torah, and it's my name. Interestingly, Pinchas takes on a new persona in a Midrash which takes off from the biblical Yiftach story. In the Book of Judges, Yiftach (an Israelite general on the eve of battle) pledges to sacrifice the first thing to walk out of his barn if God brings him victory. He defeats the Philistines, but his daughter is the first to emerge from

---

14. Rashi on Numbers 25:12.

the barn. In the Midrash, Yiftach petitioned Caleb – the secular leader – and Pinchas – now the high priest – to annul his vow. But both leaders felt that it was beneath them to travel to Yiftach, so they insisted that Yiftach visit them personally before they would annul the vow. Yiftach, however, thought it beneath him to travel to those leaders, so he ended up killing his daughter.

It's an odd transformation for Pinchas – from lonely zealot to ego-driven bureaucrat. But maybe that's the lesson. Maybe ego is ultimately at the root of all fanaticism, and Pinchas teaches us, through his cautionary example, that aging fanatics inevitably become corrupt and cruel. Or maybe we can learn how easy it is, in any giving profession, to lose our fiery concern for others, and divert our attention to ourselves. I may have to content myself with seeing Pinchas as a negative mirror, a model of what *not* to become. As a young man, he believed in something, but by the end, he only believed in himself.

Mattot-Massei – Spiritual Renewal

In the first portion of this week's double reading, the Torah commands that soldiers who have killed others in battle must undergo a seven-day purification ritual. The commandment is odd, since no one is accusing these soldiers of a crime, or of any immoral action which might "pollute" their souls. Sometimes wars are necessary, and the Torah guides as to when it's proper to fight. So why, in a properly constituted war, blame the soldiers for killing others? It's also strange that both the Torah and Rashi use the term *niddah* in discussing the soldiers. A *niddah* is a menstruating woman who must also undergo a nearly identical purification ritual. Again, there's no suggestion that the woman is to blame for menstruating, or that her actions have somehow made her impure. So why does she need to purify herself? And why is a fighting soldier compared to a menstruating woman?

The key here is not moral blame, but spiritual renewal. It's true that a soldier is not morally or judicially guilty of a crime when killing another soldier, but from an emotional or spiritual point of view, the soldier has definitely experienced a trauma, and probably needs renewal. Similarly, a menstruating woman, especially in ancient times, experiences a kind of loss, since the blood of menstruation powerfully symbolizes a lost pregnancy. Again, from the point of view of morality, there's no question of blame. But when something's lost, even a potential pregnancy, there's an emotional or spiritual cost.

The second portion of our double reading describes the cities of refuge, where accidental killers flee. On the one hand, this remarkable institution simply provides shelter for the non-culpable killer, a place where the "blood redeemer" – the victim's nearest relative – cannot enter and extract revenge. But the Talmud looked at cities of refuge as prisons, and even our reading suggests that there's more going on than just shelter. The killer is allowed to leave after the High Priest dies, implying that, in addition to shelter, the killer needed time. Again, there's no question here of moral or criminal culpability; the Torah makes it quite clear that the killer is not guilty of any crime. But there's an emotional or spiritual consequence to taking another life.

I recently read a book by noted law professor, Thane Rosenbaum, in which he points out that our American legal system works well in solving criminal and even moral issues, but still leaves many of us emotionally dissatisfied. A jury can rule a killer "not guilty" because of self-defense, but that judicial ruling, for all its moral clarity, doesn't end the story. The killer took a life. There's no need for punishment, but there's almost certainly a need for renewal. The Torah, even in its supposedly "legalistic" chapters, is never just concerned with right and wrong, with guilt or innocence. The Torah's biggest concern, in fact, is repair, or renewal. A soldier doing his duty is not guilty of a crime. But he may need space, time, and ritual before reentering his life.

Chapter 5

DEUTERONOMY

Devarim – Move Forward

This week's reading, which opens the book of Deuteronomy, contains two important, though often overlooked, passages. Chapter 2, verse 1 tells us that in the aftermath of the incident with the spies, the people headed toward the desert and "circled Mount Seir for many days." In the next verse, God tells the people: "Enough circling this mountain! Turn North." How long were the people circling Mount Seir? Rashi and other commentators give us the obvious, though startling, answer: 38 years! After informing us that the people "circled Mount Seir," the Torah is silent for 38 years, picking up where God tells the people to stop running in circles.

Why were they running in circles for 38 years? One answer is that the incident of the spies – and the aftermath, where many Israelites died in battle, and God punished the entire community by refusing them entry into Israel – so traumatized the people that they acted like chickens with their heads cut off – circling aimlessly.

Another deeper possibility is that they didn't want to face what came next. And what was that? One answer is the responsibilities of being a free people in their own land. But the Torah itself is more specific; God tells them that their next task is to confront "your brothers, the people of Esau."[1]

The Israelites had been avoiding Esau since the original feud between Jacob (aka Israel) and his twin brother Esau. God is now telling the Israelites that it's time to stop avoiding Esau; it's time to face the estranged brother.

This could mean that it is also time to embrace Esau's characteristics. In Genesis, Jacob (Israel) is spiritual and intellectual, while Esau is physical and impulsive. God could be telling the people that now that they will rule a land of their own, they will need to embrace Esau-like characteristics. They'll need to become more physical, less intellectual.

But it could also mean that it's time to engage seriously with the people of Esau. Jacob's feud with Esau, which became our feud with Esau's descendants, has the Israelites running in place, avoiding obvious, if painful, solutions. God tells the people to stop running in circles. The status quo only exacerbates the conflict, leading to greater misunderstandings, and deeper enmity.

These days, I can imagine God's voice speaking to both us and the Palestinians, two peoples locked in a fratricidal conflict, for which the solutions are painfully obvious. Enough circling around the problem, God tells us. Move forward.

Va'etchanan – To Love is to Give

This week's reading contains both the Ten Commandments, our most important ethical and spiritual instructions, and the *Shema*, our most important prayer. The second line of the *Shema* commands us, famously, to "love" God with all our heart, soul, and might. This commandment presents several difficulties. One, it's hard to imagine loving anything on command. For modern people, love, like all emotions, is either something that pops up spontaneously or develops involuntarily, over time. How can anyone command me how to feel?

---

1.   Deuteronomy 2:4.

Two, it's specifically difficult (though, of course, not impossible) to imagine loving God. The Torah describes a highly abstract, invisible, God, one we're not allowed to symbolize with concrete images. Pagans can use stones or trees to focus their emotions on God, and even Christians can use the image of a man on a cross. But the Torah leaves us with very few concrete tools for imagining God, and it's hard to love anything we can't imagine.

The lines following the *Shema*, concerning the land of Israel, help us understand how to love God, by showing us how God gives love to us. Moses says that God will give the people "great cities that you did not build, and houses filled with goodness that you did not fill, dug wells that you did not dig, and vineyards and olive groves that you did not plant."[2] God emphasizes here that the land of Israel is a pure gift, something the people did nothing to deserve. God shows us love, in other words, by gracing us with undeserved gifts, such as lungs for breathing that we did not form, grass to walk on that we did not plant, the sun to warm us that we did not create. In return, we love God by offering the gift of a full and gracious obedience to His commandments. We love God by giving; God loves us by giving us precisely those precious gifts that we do nothing to warrant.

In addition to clarifying how to love God, these lines teach important general lessons about both love and giving. The gifts we should most appreciate, according to our reading, are those we don't deserve, because these are acts of pure love. And, in Judaism, to love is to give. The two concepts are nearly synonymous.

Ekev – What God Expects

This week's reading includes Moses' famous charge to the Israelites: "What does God expect from you but fear of God [*yir'ah*, which can mean either 'fear' or 'awe.']"[3] This wording implies that God doesn't expect very much from us at all. But the Talmud asks,

---

2. Ibid. 6:10–11.
3. Ibid. 10:12.

reasonably, is *yir'ah* really such a small thing? Rabbi Yossi answers that for Moses, a spiritual genius, *yir'ah*, is, in fact, a small thing, but for us, it's something that requires great effort and offers great rewards in return.

The Ishbitzer Rebbe compares *yir'ah* to bread. He points out that we don't describe a rich person as having a lot of bread; we understand that bread would be the least of a rich person's possessions. But we do describe poor people as not owning even a crust of bread. In other words, for a rich person, bread is no big deal, but for a poor person, it looms quite large, because it's what keeps us alive from day to day.

When it comes to *yir'ah*, which I'd define now as "awe," most of us suffer from great poverty, even if we're not aware of it. Scientific materialism has stolen much of the awe from modern life. When we look at clouds, for example, or contemplate our dreams, we're more likely to consider their scientific origins than stand in awe of the mysteries these phenomena both hide and reveal.

But a sense of awe is the minimal requirement for a religious life, a life connected to God. The great Jewish philosopher A.J. Heschel used to point to beggars in Manhattan and tell whoever was walking with him, "You see that man. If you look closely, you can see the face of God." He meant, of course, that all of life, in its stunning complexity, should fill us with *yir'ah*, a sense of awe and wonder.

While snorkeling recently in Hawaii, I was reminded, while swimming among the colorful coral and beautifully complex tropical fish, of God's infinite capacity for creativity. I was filled with a sense of wonder that I hope I brought back with me from vacation, as I contemplate the more mundane world. In our reading, Moses instructs me, and everyone else, that I need to develop this *yir'ah* as an absolute minimum for living a truly religious life. Unfortunately, for me at least, Moses is asking a lot.

Re'eh – Finding Our Prophets

This week's reading includes several verses warning the people about false prophets. The Torah is teaching us here that even if prophets perform genuine miracles, we should not listen to them if they tell us to stray from God's word.

In the course of ancient Jewish history, these passages had the effect, if not the intent, of discouraging prophets from revealing themselves. It's in the nature of prophets to suggest changes in the status quo (why else would a prophet be needed?). But any Israelite tyrant could use these verses (for example, "Do not heed the words of that prophet...for the Lord your God is testing you"[4]) as an excuse to arrest and even execute a prophet who, in violation of the Torah, advocated disobeying the king. In fact, many true prophets, including Elijah and Jeremiah, were persecuted, on the basis of these verses.

The verses themselves point to a fascinating transition in Jewish history, where authority moves from charismatic miracle-working holy men to earth-bound scholars. Both God and Moses originally derive all authority from their ability to perform miracles. God explicitly states that He brings "signs and wonders"[5] to Egypt to convince people to worship Him. Moses becomes a "great man"[6] in Egypt by using his staff to bring on the plagues.

But the verses in this week's reading discourage miracle workers from becoming leaders. And the rabbis of the Mishnah and Talmud actually forbade prophets from rendering legal decisions. Rabbis derived their authority from their mastery of sacred texts, not from the supernatural. They were scholars and teachers, not holy men.

Unfortunately, Judaism, as a spiritual system, suffered because of the loss of holy men (and women) as leaders. The Hasidic movement, in part, arose in response to the human yearning to seek out spiritual geniuses, leaders whose actions and teachings reflect an immediate closeness to God, rather than scholastic competence.

4. Deuteronomy 13:4
5. Exodus 7:3.
6. Ibid. 11.3.

Today, the Jewish world needs to embrace both Torah scholars and charismatic holy men and women (some great leaders, of course, have both qualities). To me, one of the great tragedies of the non-Orthodox world is the way we've treated Reb Zalman Schachter, one of Judaism's great spiritual geniuses of our age. Although Reb Zalman has influenced thousands of students, he never taught at a major rabbinical school, and was never appreciated or supported by mainstream congregations. He's now ending his career at the Naropa Institute – a Buddhist institution – where he teaches Hasidic wisdom to Buddhists. We need to find a way to re-introduce the "holy man" into Jewish leadership so we don't overlook the next Reb Zalman.

Shoftim – Faith in Divine Justice

This week's reading includes the laws concerning the future appointment of an Israelite king. There's a fascinating ambivalence in these passages. The phrasing of the commandment indicates that, while the people clearly will want a king, God will have reservations. And, in fact, much later in Jewish history, when the people approach the prophet Samuel and ask for a king, he, on God's behalf, protests their request. God, after all, is the true Sovereign.

So, why would the people want a king? Most commentators answer that during Samuel's time, Israel was threatened by the Philistines, and needed a strong warrior. But that's only half the answer. It's clear from our reading that a king also represents an alternative judicial authority – a strong man who will rule decisively. The verses preceding the laws of the king describe a judicial system where priests consult God and then render legal decisions. The priests derive their authority, as clergy, from God. Kings, on the other hand, derive their authority from the power of the state. They have the ability to rule decisively and back up their rulings with the force of an army.

According to the Midrash, the people approached Samuel and asked for a king after a priest had allowed a murderer to go free. The only witnesses to the crime were heretics, so the priest disqualified the witnesses, freeing the killer. The people were so horrified that a murderer got off scott-free, they demanded a king, who presumably would never release criminals on technicalities.

Clearly, this was an issue of faith. The priests were confident that, although they were releasing the killer from the human justice system, God, in the fullness of time, would punish him, either in this life or the next. The people, on the other hand, didn't share the priests' faith. Rather, they felt anxiety over a system which, potentially, allowed the guilty to go free.

Our society today also experiences anxiety over our judicial system. Many Americans have lost confidence in our judicial system, because they see guilty people getting away with various crimes. We also have a genuine concern that killers may be roaming the streets, waiting for their next target. But for me, this is also a question of faith. In my opinion, we have become disappointed in our judicial system because we expect too much from it. In fact, all human legal systems will fail at some point to create absolute justice.

But we, like our ancient priests, should have the faith that, sooner or later, God punishes the guilty. Paradoxically, a stronger faith in God will lead to a healthier confidence in our human courts and judges.

Ki Tetsei – Small Acts of Kindness

This is a difficult reading to study. It features several harsh penalties and nasty crimes, including stoning, rape, adultery, child abuse, and many other manifestations of human ugliness. Our first temptation is to turn away from these subjects, though we have to admit that these things exist; the reading portrays the world accurately.

In the middle of the ugliness (specifically between child abuse and adultery), the Torah presents a moment of mercy and decency. When taking eggs from a nest, the Torah commands us to send away the mother bird, presumably so she won't have to witness the loss of her child. The lesson here seems to be that we can strive for basic decency even under harsh circumstances. Interestingly, some Talmudic rabbis question whether the purpose of sending away the mother bird is indeed to show mercy to the mother. They resist any attempt to understand God's motivations. We perform commandments, they insist, simply because God instructs us.

In commenting on this commandment, Maimonides quotes these rabbis, but, amazingly, writes "*We* think otherwise." Maimonides insists that the mother bird would feel great pain at seeing someone snatch away her eggs. He implies that others (those Talmudic rabbis) resist searching for mercy in an ugly world, but "we" understand our obligations to act decently, even under the worst circumstances. We know what God wants when the world falls apart.

Many of us were stunned and depressed at the scenes of looting and other lawlessness that followed Hurricane Katrina. And it's true that, for some people, awful circumstances provoke our nihilistic "dark" side. But for every rape and murder in Louisiana, there were countless more acts of basic decency – neighbors risking their lives to rescue their neighbors; strangers sharing food with strangers; doctors, nurses, and policemen staying behind to help out; rescue workers comforting crying, lost children. The authentic ugliness all around us can sometimes blind us to the greater beauty. But dark circumstances shouldn't rob us of human decency or our ability to act out God's great mercy.

Ki Tavo – Living with Anxiety

In the latest Bob Dylan album, there's a line where a character sings: "The sun is strong, I'm standing in the light/ I wish to God that it were night." It's a powerful lyric because it describes a paradoxical feeling that's strangely familiar to all of us: a joyous, sacred moment, followed by dissatisfaction. We can't hold onto the happiness because of our anxiety for the future. In the song, it's because the singer is pining over Nettie Moore, his lost love. This chronic emptiness forces him to shuffle in and out of redemptive moments.

It's quite possible that Dylan borrowed the line from a verse in this week's reading, a curse which says: "In the morning you'll say 'If only it were evening,' and in the evening you'll say 'If only it were morning.'" These words convey a powerful lesson on how we might misuse the spirit of Rosh Hashanah and Yom Kippur. On the surface, the High Holidays encourage standing in the light, but wishing it were night. Rosh Hashanah and particularly Yom Kippur urge us to scrutinize our lives critically, and discover pathways towards change. Under their power, we cast suspicious glances at the status quo, even the good parts. After all, we can't yearn for a better future unless we disavow the present.

But the Torah (and, I suppose, Bob Dylan) teaches us that there's a thin line between wishing for change and chronic dissatisfaction; between hope and anxiety. Yom Kippur may propel us toward change, and this is certainly right and healthy. But perpetual anxiety can drive us all crazy.

For the Dylan character, it's lost love which drives him crazy, giving him the feeling that the present is never good enough, even when it's filled with light. For the Torah, it's fear that moves us beyond simple hope into constant apprehension. The full verse states: "In the morning you'll say 'If only it were evening,' and in the evening you'll say 'If only it were morning,' out of the *fear* that it's in your heart." All of us, deep down, carry fears that we will lose those people and things we need the most – our jobs, our homes, our health, our most significant relationships. This fear can easily drive us towards constant self-examination – a relentless inventory of everything that might go wrong, and snatch away all that is precious to us. Simple hope for change becomes a frenetic obsession with improvement, just so we won't lose those fragile things that we need. This is the Torah's curse, wishing it were night, even during the day.

The solution, of course, is both recognizing our fear, and learning to live with it. A healthy soul yearns for change, but also learns to let go – to put the fate of everything we need and love in God's hands, for better or for worse. Fear robs us of our capacity to enjoy and appreciate the present. It forces us to change simply for the sake of change. It makes us wish it were night while standing in the light.

Nitzavim-Vayelech – Repentance for All

This week's reading, the first in the Bible to teach *"teshuvah,"* or repentance (or "return") as an authentic spiritual option, suggests that the process hinges on hearing God's voice. What does it mean to hear God's voice, and then return to a better life? I might interpret this as an inner voice, flowing from a profound spiritual consciousness, which whispers to us a way out of our damaging behavior. According to the Midrash, there's a voice that cries out every day "Return you backsliding children" (a line from Jeremiah). We chant this line several times during the Yom Kippur service, as a kind of echo to the heavenly voice which cries to us every day, but that we often fail to hear.

There's a wonderful story in the Talmud about a sinner and apostate, Rabbi Elisha ben Abuyah. The Talmud refers to him as *"Acher,"* meaning "the other" or "someone else," because once, shortly after choosing a life of sin, he approached a prostitute on Shabbat. Shocked, the young woman said: "Aren't you the famous Rabbi Elisha?" He responded by tearing a leaf, a clear Shabbat violation. She said, "Oh, it must be *acher* ('someone else')." One day, Elisha's former student Rabbi Meir begged him to repent. Elisha answered, "I once heard a voice shout out: 'Return you backsliding children – except *Acher*.'"

Elisha, of course, is referring to the voice that's available to all of us, the voice announcing the great human capacity – with God's help – to change, to repent. But Elisha heard this voice differently; he heard that everyone else in the world has the capacity to change, but not him, because he's *"Acher,"* he's different; he's someone else.

Elisha may be referring here to his own megalomania; he may be claiming to be above any and all rules. Other people need to change, he may be saying, but not me. But my sense is that Elisha is experiencing a deeper kind of *acher* – an alienation that flows from despair. He's saying that others can change because their situations are not as hopeless as mine. I'm different, he's saying; I'm *acher*, in that I'm in too deep; my crisis is too daunting.

And that's precisely the type of *acher* that we need to combat during the time of the High Holidays, whether we find it in ourselves, or in loved ones. Because, as the Midrash teaches, the voice is always there. God gives everyone, without exception, the innate capacity to change. Our dignity as human beings lies in our ability to forge new paths, or to retrace our steps, and return. The one thing that all human beings share is the ability to change our behavior. In this sense, none of us is *acher*; none of us is different; none of us is alone.

Ha'azinu – Finding God

There are many passages in this week's reading which suggest that approaching God is a struggle, requiring sustained effort. For example, Moses opens our reading by proclaiming: "Give ear, O Heavens, let me speak; let the Earth hear the words I utter." Most commentators define the command "Give ear" as a call to listen from close up, as opposed to "hear," which is a request to listen from a distance. Since Moses uses the phrase "give ear" when talking to Heaven, we can assume that, at this point in his career, Moses is closer to God than he is to human beings. Rashi and many other scholars claim that Moses only became especially close to Heaven towards the end of his life because of his great work in leading the Jewish people, and because of his advanced age.

This verse serves as a jumping-off point in the Midrash for a discussion on how to become close to God. One rabbi suggests that building the Land of Israel brings us up "to Heaven." Another says that it's the offering of sacrifices (or prayer). A third says it's study; a fourth says cultivating a sense of belonging to the Jewish people brings us "to Heaven." All four agree that we only approach God closely through specific, intense actions.

However, another verse suggests otherwise. Towards the end of his speech, Moses, quoting God, says, "See then that I, I am He. There is no God but Me. I kill and I bring life. I wound and I heal. There is no escape from Me."[7] This verse insists that God is an inevitable presence in our lives, whether we work for it or not; in fact, whether we like it or not. What does it mean when God says "there is no escape from Me?" Rabbi Harold Schullweiss writes that one definition of God is: "the reality principle in the Universe." God, in other words, invents and governs the physical laws which bring us great pleasure, but which also sometimes cause us pain, and from which there really is no escape. Furthermore, our guilty consciences, especially when we read this portion between Rosh Hashanah and Yom Kippur, prove that even in the privacy of our own thoughts, there's no escape from God's moral laws. Jonah, in the Yom Kippur *Haftorah*, learns this lesson well.

Obviously, building a relationship with God is complicated. On the one hand, we labor our whole lives to approach God intimately. On the other hand, there will be times when we'd just as soon avoid confronting God, but there will be no escape.

Zot Ha'berachah: A Blessing for Me?

Blessings. A good way to end both books. In the Torah's first book, God's first act after creating the world is to offer words of blessing, first to the "swarms of living creatures" from the sky and the sea, and then to the first human beings. Moses' last act, in the last chapter of the Torah's last book, is to bless the tribes. One gets the impression that the Torah is a book filled with blessings.

But that's not quite true. Blessing is certainly an important theme in the Torah, but its application is somewhat limited. For example, God never actually blesses Abraham. God tells him that He will, in the future, "bless him," and that "whoever blesses [him] will be blessed,"[8] but there's no scene in which God actually

7. Deuteronomy 32:39.
8. Genesis 12:2–3.

confers words of blessing on Abraham, no line beginning "God blessed Abraham." An angel blesses him after the *Akeidah* (the Binding of Isaac), but not God.

Abraham himself never blesses his children. God also never blesses Isaac. Joseph never blesses his children, neither does Moses bless his sons (and, of course, Moses' father never blesses him). Moses "charges" his successor Joshua, but he doesn't bless him. God instructs Aaron how priests will bless the people in the future, but Aaron, himself, never blesses the people. Later in the Tanach, after the first five books, the word "blessing" almost disappears entirely. At his deathbed, King David, like Jacob, tries to impart wisdom to his son. But the Bible here uses the word *ve-yitzav* (commanded), not *vayivarech* (blessed).

It's actually the patriarch Jacob who, like a large planet exerting an immense gravitational force, attracts most of the blessing activity in the Bible. He steals his brother's blessing, deceiving his father in the process. He physically wrests a blessing from an angel. He's the only character whom God (not an angel) explicitly blesses, and this is an incident Jacob recalls late in his life. He blesses all his sons (well, he tries. I'll get to that in a moment). He blesses Joseph's sons even though Joseph doesn't bless them himself. He even blesses Pharaoh, twice. And now, in our reading, we have Moses' blessing, but this is another blessing of Jacob's sons, their names now adorning the tribes of Israel. It's as if Jacob, long dead, is still pulling in blessings.

The most provocative rabbinic comment I found regarding Moses' blessing is from this Midrash: "Moses began his blessings from the place where Jacob concluded." In fact, the rabbis characterized Jacob's blessing of his sons as a *birkat satum* – a hard phrase to translate, but it means something like a "blocked," or "limited," or "incomplete" blessing. In the Midrash, Jacob lost his prophetic powers just as he began to bless his oldest sons. That explains why his first blessings are more like rebukes than blessings; they offer few good wishes, and they don't predict the future. Jacob regained his powers for his younger sons, but the blessing as a whole remains *satum*, blocked, incomplete.

Moses, of course, dies at the height of his powers, so, according to the Midrash, he completes Jacob's blessing, by accurately prophesying exactly what's going to happen. The Kli Yakar also suggests that Moses improves on Jacob's blessing by giving some of the tribes a little more than they received from their father. For example, Joseph goes from being an "ass" (*ben porat*) to an "ox" (*shor*). He also goes from someone who is attacked by arrows to someone who "gores."

I might suggest that Moses doesn't actually perfect or improve on Jacob, but merely moves the blessings into the future, so they're consistent with their time and space. Moses' modest blessing of Reuben, for instance – "May Reuben live and not die" – doesn't seem like much an improvement over Jacob's "My might and first of my vigor." But the tribe of Reuben had clearly grown weak at this point, and what they needed most was survival. Also, Jacob never blessed Simon; he rebuked him. But Moses leaves him out altogether, leaving us with the chilling impression that his tribe had disappeared completely, lost in the desert battles. This is certainly no improvement, but it's reality, and it's appropriate to this time and space. We see Moses here continuing Jacob's work, but not just in the sense of improving on his ancestor's blessings. Moses reminds us that, as the people of Jacob, we are a people of blessing. We need to bless each other.

What exactly is a blessing? For the rabbis, it appears to be a prophetic pronouncement – a wish for the future that will come true simply because it's pronounced. That's why the rabbis called Jacob's blessing *satum*, not because he wasn't articulate, or because he didn't love his sons, but because he was a blocked prophet.

But what's a blessing for me? In my contemporary Jewish practice, it means ritually bestowing words of encouragement. Not, in other words, saying "good job!" or "cheer up," but laying on my hands, at fixed times, and offering ritual words of encouragement, while invoking God.

My parents never blessed me. This isn't a complaint (well, maybe it is, a little), because they certainly *encouraged* me, and expressed their good wishes and hopes in hundreds of other ways. They simply never laid their hands on me while invoking God. It wasn't our family practice.

Another way of putting it, though (and this *is* a complaint): my parents' blessing was *satum*; it was blocked, incomplete. My mother's suicide attempt, the affairs, the divorce, bouncing from place to place, their early deaths: all these things, in some way, *blocked* the flow of their love. There was something missing. There still is.

As it happens, I do bless my children, every Friday night. I put my hands on their heads, and whisper the words Jacob offered to his grandchildren. Today, the day I write this, is Friday. Tonight I'll bless my sons, Benjamin and Ilan.

Biography

Biographical Details of Famous Jewish Thinkers and Rabbis Throughout the Ages Noted in This Work

Rashi. 1040–1105. Rabbi Shlomo Yitzhaki. Greatest Jewish biblical commentator, from Troyes, France.

Maimonides. 1135–1204. Rabbi Moshe ben Maimon. One of the greatest Jewish thinkers of all time. Active mostly in Spain and Egypt.

Nachmanides. 1194–1270. Rabbi Moshe ben Nachman. Great biblical commentator and Jewish communal leader in Spain.

Bartenura. Late 1400s. Rabbi Ovadiah of Bartenura. Foremost explicator of the Mishnah and Pirkei Avot ("Sayings of the Fathers").

Kli Yakar. 1560–1619. Ephraim Solomon of Luntschitz. Great biblical commentator from Poland.

Ohr HaChayim. 1696–1743. Rabbi Chaim ben Moshe ibn Attar. Mystic and biblical commentator, active in Morocco and Israel.

Vilna Gaon. 1720–1797. Rabbi Elijah of Vilna. The *gaon* ("genius") of Vilna, one of the greatest Talmudic thinkers of all time.

Levi Isaac of Berdichev. 1740–1810. Early Hasidic Master, who taught in Britchval, Zelichav, and Pinsk, as well as Berdichev.

The Ishbitzer Rebbe. 1800–1854. Rabbi Mordechai Yoseph, also known as the Mei HaShiloach ("Living Waters"). Founder of the Ishbitz Hasidic dynasty.

The Gerrer Rebbe. 1847–1905. Rabbi Yehuda Leib Alter, also known as the Sefas Emes ("Language of Truth"). Founder of the Ger Hasidic dynasty, at its time the largest Hasidic group in Poland.

Rav Kook. 1864–1935. Rabbi Abraham Isaac Kook. Great mystic and poet, as well as the first Ashkenazic Chief Rabbi of Mandatory Palestine.

A.J. Heschel. 1907–1972. Born to a Hasidic family, became a longtime professor of mysticism at the Jewish Theological Seminary in New York.

Reb Zalman Schachter. Great contemporary teacher of Torah, mostly associated with the Jewish Renewal movement.

Aviva Zornberg. One of the greatest contemporary teachers of Torah. Author of several books of biblical commentary.